ROCK THAT
QUILT BLOCK

ROCK THAT
QUILT BLOCK

10 Gorgeous Quilts to Make from the Country Crown Block

Linda J. Hahn
& Deborah G. Stanley

Landauer Publishing

Rock That Quilt Block

Landauer Publishing, *www.landauerpub.com*, is an imprint of
Fox Chapel Publishing Company, Inc.

Copyright © 2020 by Linda J. Hahn, Deborah G. Stanley, and
Fox Chapel Publishing Company, Inc., 903 Square Street, Mount Joy,
PA 17552.

Project Team
Acquisition Editor: Tiffany Hill
Editor: Katie Ocasio
Copy Editor: Anthony Regolino
Designer: Wendy Reynolds
Photographer: Mike Mihalo
Indexer: Jay Kreider

ISBN 978-1-947163-34-8

Library of Congress Cataloging-in-Publication Data

Names: Hahn, Linda, author. | Stanley, Deborah G., author.
Title: Rock that quilt block / Linda J. Hahn and Deborah G. Stanley.
Other titles: Rock that quilt block (Landauer Publishing)
Description: Mount Joy : Landauer Publishing, [2020] | Includes
  index. | Summary: "Contains information on how to create the
  Country Crown quilt block, as well as various combinations you
  can do to create different patterns. Also includes step-by-step
  projects with illustrations"— Provided by publisher.
Identifiers: LCCN 2019054576 (print) | LCCN 2019054577
  (ebook) | ISBN 9781947163348 (paperback) | ISBN
  9781607657972 (ebook)
Subjects: LCSH: Patchwork—Patterns. | Quilting—Patterns.
Classification: LCC TT835 .H25825 2020 (print) | LCC TT835
  (ebook) | DDC 746.46/041—dc23
LC record available at https://lccn.loc.gov/2019054576
LC ebook record available at https://lccn.loc.gov/2019054577

We are always looking for talented authors. To submit an idea,
please send a brief inquiry to acquisitions@foxchapelpublishing.com.

Printed in Singapore
23 22 21 20   2 4 6 8 10 9 7 5 3 1

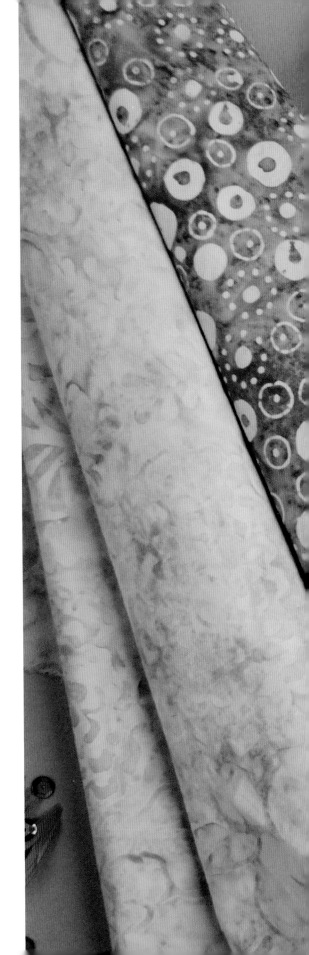

Batik fabrics, such as Linda Hahn's Canivale fabric collection by Banyan Batiks seen here, are great for creating the colorful quilts in this book.

Contents

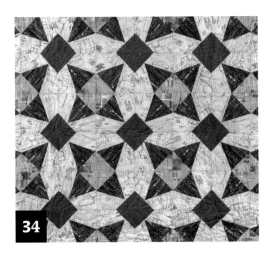

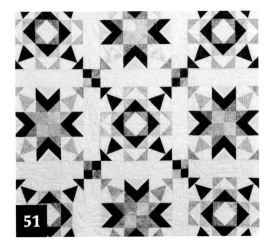

38

42

46

57

62

66

80

Foreword

Linda (left) and Deborah (right) Photo by: Bonnie McCaffrey

Hi, quilters!

We are so happy that you want to play blocks with us! We have so much fun taking a specific block or block component and exploring how you can change the whole flavor of the quilt by simply adding a color, rotating a piece, incorporating into or combining it with other simple shapes, or perhaps adding a sashing.

We hope that this book will stimulate your creative juices and get you thinking outside your box. What you learn in this book can most certainly be applied to other blocks.

Linda and Deborah

Batik fabrics are an excellent choice for adding color to your quilts.

Supplies and Materials

Let's start off by talking about the different types of supplies and materials you'll need for making the quilts in this book.

Rotary Equipment

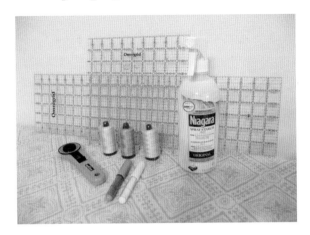

- **Rotary cutter:** Choose your favorite rotary cutter with a nice sharp blade; a sharp blade ensures clean and accurate cuts.
- **Rulers:** We use the Omnigrid® 9½" (24.13-cm) square ruler (it fits perfectly in your hand and can also go into a purse or bag) and an Omnigrid 6" x 24" (15.24- x 60.96-cm) ruler. It's always best to stick with the same brand of ruler throughout your project for consistency.
- **Rotary cutting gadgets:** Items such as gloves, handles, stabilizers, etc., are all more of a personal preference, so we will not expand on those too much.

Thread

We use—and highly recommend—Aurifil 50 wt. thread for piecing. We use neutral colors such as beige, taupe, or light gray. Do not use metallic thread, quilting thread, or very old thread for piecing.

Marking Tools

We prefer marking tools that are chalk based, as we think they are easier to work with. To this end, we like the Clover Chaco Liner.

What's My Angle Tool

Buying a seam guide that you can tape to your machine and use over and over again, like the What's My Angle tool, is highly recommended. You can make HSTs and connector squares without having to mark your fabric. (See Resources, page 87.)

Triangles on a Roll™

When we have to make a lot of HST, we will use Triangles on a Roll. It definitely helps things move along much quicker. (See Resources, page 87.)

Foundation Paper

CHOOSING YOUR PAPER

There are many different types of foundation paper on the market, and you are welcome to use the paper of your choice. Our paper of preference is, of course, our foundation paper (see Resources, page 87), which we like because it can be left in the quilt, meaning no more ripping out the paper.

Frog Hollow Designs foundation paper will soften up over time, and will become a thin layer of polyester inside the quilt if washed. It can also go through your printer. We like that it can be left in the quilt, which means no more ripping out paper.

If you choose another type of foundation paper, we recommend using a vellum or translucent foundation paper. The translucent paper is what makes this technique so easy, rather than the standard printer paper.

If you are using foundation paper that must be removed, do not remove it until you have stitched the block into the quilt. To remove, you can spritz the area with water to soften up the paper and make it easier to remove, or lightly run a pin down the center to "score" the paper and it will rip out.

COPIER DISTORTION (IT HAPPENS!)

- **Consistency**: All copiers are not created equal. Before you copy your entire package of foundation paper, make one copy of the pattern and check the measurements. This applies not just to the patterns in this book but to every foundation paper pattern that you may use. If you copy something at home but decide to switch to a new copier, you may find that the copies are not the same size. Copy all the patterns on the same copier for continuity.
- **Scanning**: Pay attention if you choose this option. Make sure that when you print the pattern, you are printing the actual size and not "fit to page."
- **Alternative to copying**: You may wish to consider the *Rock That Quilt Block* kit available on our website (see Resources, page 87), which contains a laser-cut, reusable foundation stencil. Trace the pattern onto the foundation paper using a Pigma® pen.

Using a handle on your ruler will make rotary cutting quick and easy.

Choosing Fabrics

Fabric choices are, of course, very personal; however, we do have some helpful hints for you.

For the most part, directional fabric for the triangle sides will not work well. Directional fabric is okay for the center triangle shape, as well as the top and bottom triangle shapes. Directional fabric could also be used for the base fabric on the Flying Geese shape and the base fabric for the SIS.

To Starch or Not to Starch

As with many things, starching is a personal preference. We prefer to starch our fabrics prior to cutting, and then also during the stitching process. After stitching a seam, spritz the pieces lightly with starch and press the seam closed—and then open the seam and press again, perhaps even doing another light mist. It is our opinion that you will get a nicer press and crease to the fabric with starching.

Spray starch will allow you to achieve crisper lines while ironing.

There are so many options to choose from. Our preference is Niagara® Pump Spray—which allows you to really direct a concentrated stream at a seam or crease.

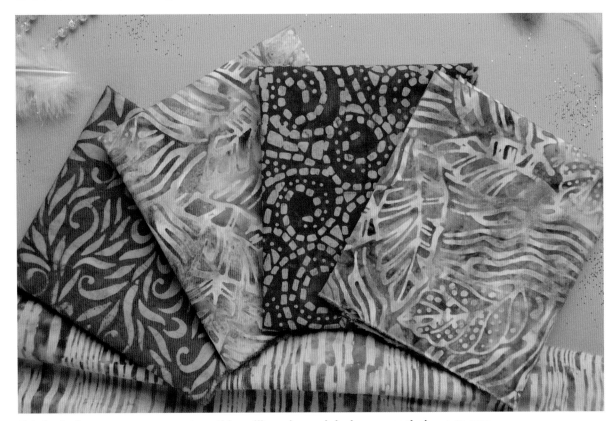

Fabric choices are very personal, so things like color and design are entirely up to you.

Prewashing

Here's another area of personal preference. Some people prefer to prewash to determine if the fabrics will bleed. Some people like the "feel" of unwashed fabric. This, dear friends, we will leave up to you.

Backing Fabric Calculations

Most people are machine quilting nowadays. A good many of those people send their quilts to a longarm quilter rather than attempt it themselves. Our backing fabric requirements take this into consideration.

Quilt backs should be at least 4" (10.15cm) wider than the quilt top on EACH SIDE.

To simplify your life, add 10" (25.4cm) to the finished measurement. This allows you to have some extra fabric at the top to load the quilt, and then at the bottom. You will also have enough fabric to make a matching hanging sleeve. If you do not care for a matching sleeve, you can calculate the backing requirements by simply adding 6" (15.25cm) to the finished size of the quilt.

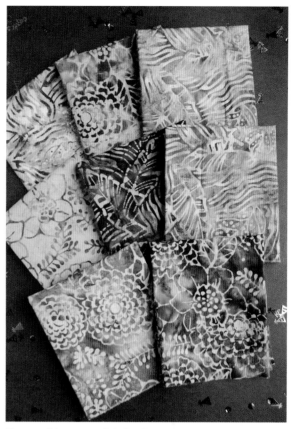

Prewashing your fabrics is a personal choice.

Seaming the Backing Fabric

Vertical seams work best, especially if you are having your quilt longarm quilted. If you use a horizontal seam and the backing pieces are not squares or on-grain, the back seam may turn out wavy. Our backing calculations take this into consideration.

It is also not necessary to center the back seam—if the seam is off to one side, you will have a larger piece of extra fabric to use in another project.

Backing fabric should be 4" (10.15cm) larger on each side

Quilt top

Backing fabric

Backing fabric should be
10" (25.4cm) longer than quilt top

Country Crown Block

Breaking It Down

The quilt block that we will be "rocking" in this book is the Country Crown (see Barbara Brackman's *Encyclopedia of Pieced Quilt Designs*). There are many interesting designs that can be made from this block and the block components. This can be done merely by adding a color, rotating a patch, or, perhaps, just combining the units in a different orientation.

Country Crown Block

TRIANGLE CORNER UNIT

This corner piece is quite interesting and very versatile. The angled pieces on the sides of the center triangle could look a little intimidating to piece, but we will do so easily and quickly using simple foundation piecing.

FLYING GEESE UNIT

There are several variations of the Flying Geese unit that we will use. Construction is exactly the same—what will differ is the angle of the "connector" squares. Sometimes these units can be made using two HSTs—in this instance, it will be to add some additional color/fabric or for consistency in construction.

 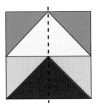

SQUARE IN A SQUARE UNIT

The Square in a Square (SIS) Center unit is also referred to as Diamond in a Square. This unit can also be made in a few different ways.

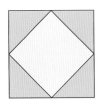 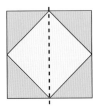 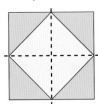

Learn the Lingo

It's important to learn the lingo we will use throughout this book for the different pieces in each block unit. After reading through this section, you'll find it much easier to understand how each part comes together to create the Country Crown block.

TRIANGLE CORNER UNIT

The block that is the focus of our play throughout this book is called the Triangle Corner unit. The Center Triangle is a 3½" x 4" (8.9 x 10.15cm) rectangle. The Triangle Sides are also 3½" x 4" (8.9 x 10.15cm) rectangles. The Top Triangle and Bottom Triangle are 3½" (8.9cm) squares cut in half on the diagonal. When stitched together, they make up the Triangle Corner unit.

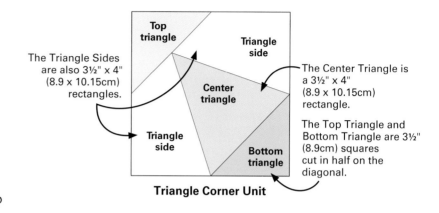

The Triangle Sides are also 3½" x 4" (8.9 x 10.15cm) rectangles.

The Center Triangle is a 3½" x 4" (8.9 x 10.15cm) rectangle.

The Top Triangle and Bottom Triangle are 3½" (8.9cm) squares cut in half on the diagonal.

Triangle Corner Unit

FLYING GEESE UNIT

The next unit that we will be using is the Flying Geese unit, and then a variation on that unit. The base fabric is the fabric that is on the bottom, and the connector units are the fabric squares that are placed on top of the base fabric. Both pieces are constructed exactly the same way, the difference being the direction that you stitch on the connector square.

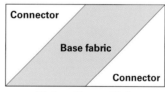
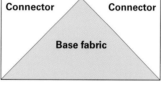

Flying Geese Unit

SQUARE IN A SQUARE UNIT

If you place a connector on each corner of a square, you will have a SIS unit.

HALF-SQUARE TRIANGLE

Finally, we also will use a quilter basic shape, the Half-Square Triangle (HST). We create our HSTs using squares as opposed to using triangles, as there is less distortion. See page 32 for a couple of different ways to make this unit, so you can choose the way you prefer.

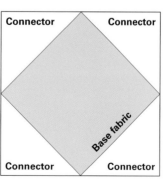
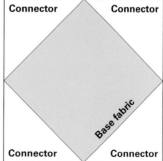

Square in a Square (SIS)   **Half-Square Triangle (HST)**

Playing with Blocks

We can do so many variations on Country Crown! Here are a few ideas that just rely on where you put the colors and how you arrange the patches within the block.

Here's the original block.

Change the color of the lower Flying Geese connectors to white.

Change the Triangle Center and Top Flying Geese units to the same color.

Make the Triangle Center and Top Flying Geese units the same color; the center is a set of HSTs in two colors.

Make the Triangle Center and Bottom Triangle units the same color, and match it to the Lower Flying Geese.

Introduce eight different colors!

Rotate the Flying Geese units, and match the Lower Flying Geese unit to the Triangle Center and Bottom Triangle units.

Make the Flying Geese units in two colors, with the Triangle Bottom units the same color as the Triangle Side units.

Make the Flying Geese units with two base colors, but use different colors on the Triangle Corner unit.

Make the Flying Geese units with one base color, but use a different color on the Triangle Bottom units.

Rotate the top Flying Geese units and add a color to the Triangle Bottom units.

Rotate the top Flying Geese units and use white Bottom Triangle units.

Rotate the top Flying Geese units and use two colors for the Flying Geese.

Rock the Center Patch Too!

You can also rock the center of the block for more variations. This one uses four HSTs in two colors.

This one uses a four-patch unit, not an SIS unit.

How to ROCK a Block

Here's how the Country Crown block turned into the quilts in this book.

1. London Underground (page 34): For this quilt, we combined four Triangle Corner units per block.

2. Elizabethan (page 38): For this quilt, we inserted a two-color thin sashing between the Triangle Corner units. Can you see that the dark background gives it a look like an iron fence? We alternated the fabrics for the triangle sides, and they look like different blocks!

3. Afternoon Tea (page 42): Tis time we changed the fabric colors and rotated the Triangle Corner units. Same block, entirely different look!

4. Countryside (page 46): This time, we added in the rest of the Country Crown block, along with a variation featuring reversed Flying Geese units.

5. Tiara (page 51): Believe it or not, this is the same quilt as the previous in different colors, but we added sashing, an additional row, and a pieced border.

6. Crown Jewels (page 57): This time, we added a 4" (10.15cm)–wide sashing, which let us bring in some additional secondary and tertiary design elements.

7. Bangers and Mash (page 62): For this quilt, we completely rearranged the components of Country Crown. Note the Triangle Corner, SIS, and Flying Geese units used throughout the quilt.

8. Kensington (page 66): This time, we did some more rotating and tried it in a different color palette.

9. Balmoral (page 74): Here's what happened when we rotated those blocks.

10. Windsor (page 80): Then we made it modern.

Techniques

Paper Piecing

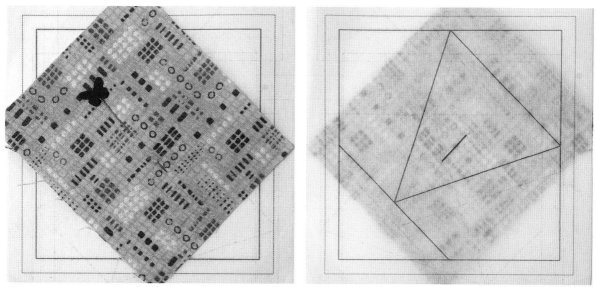

1. Place the 3½" x 4" (8.9 x 10.15cm) Triangle Center fabric RSU on the foundation paper, centering it between the triangle lines.

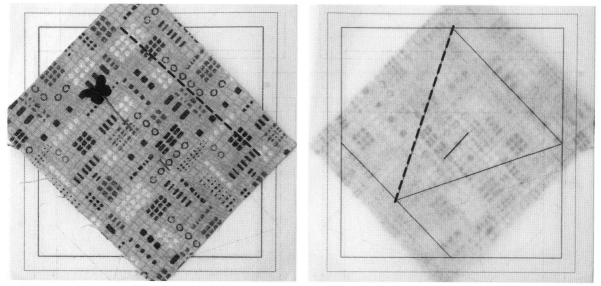

2. With the Triangle fabric RSU, fold the fabric and the paper so that you see the piecing line. Crease this line (and fabric). Following this procedure will give you the placement line for the next piece.

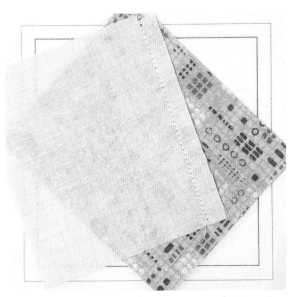

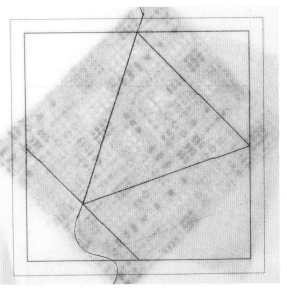

3. Place the 3½" x 4" (8.9 x 10.15cm) Triangle Side fabric RSD on the foundation paper, going over the creased line approximately ⅛" to ¼" (0.3 to 0.65cm). Make sure that the fabric covers the outermost edge of the foundation pattern.

4. Flip the pieces over and stitch from the outermost line to a few stitches beyond the tip of the triangle. Going beyond the tip by a few stitches ensures that the stitches will be anchored down by the seam that runs across the tip of the triangle.

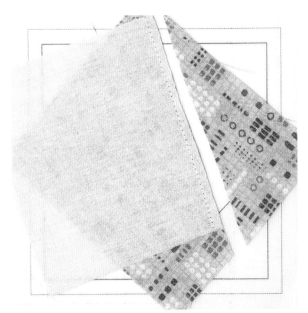

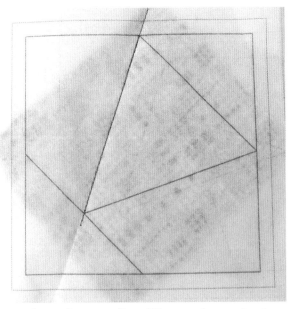

5. Trim the excess fabric approximately ⅛" (0.3cm) away from the seam line. **It's very important that you take care not to cut the paper.** Fold the piece over and repeat on the opposite side.

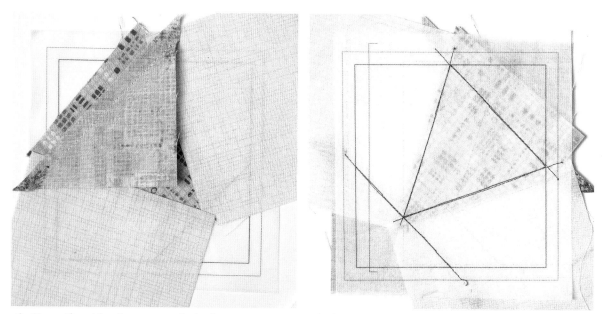

6. Once the side pieces are stitched on, you can attach the Top and Bottom Triangle pieces that are cut from the 3½" (8.9cm) squares. It does not make a difference which you attach first; it is the same procedure for both the Top and the Bottom Triangles.

Holding the foundation piece RSU, fold the paper and fabric in so that you see the triangle line. Crease this line so that you will be able to see the placement line for your triangle fabric. Place the triangle fabric approximately ⅛" to ¼" (0.3 to 0.65cm) over the creased line. Flip and stitch from one outermost line to the adjacent outermost line of the foundation paper.

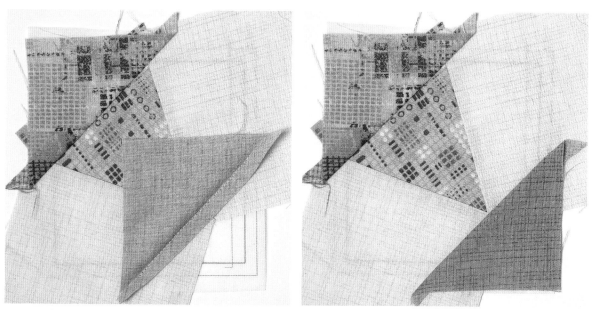

7. Attach the other triangle piece in the same way you did the first.

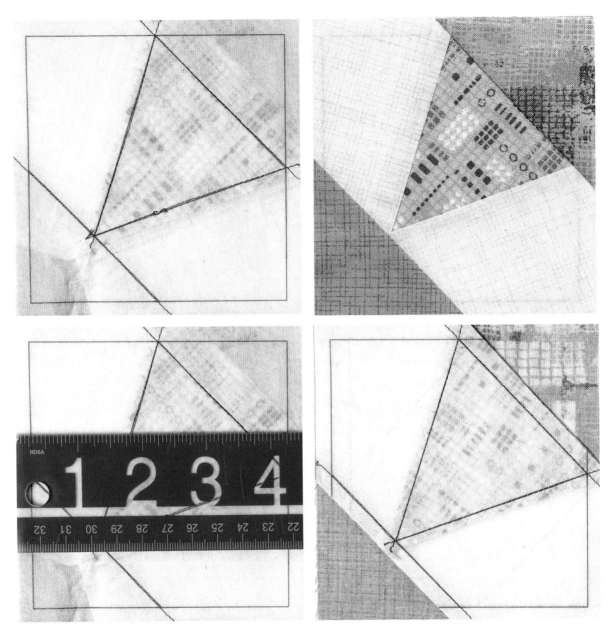

8. Your completed Corner will look like this once completed.

Trim the piece so it can be used in the quilt. It's really important that you trim the corner blocks in this order. First, turn the block over and trim to the outermost line. It must measure 4½" (11.45cm) square.

9. AFTER the block has been trimmed, carefully trim away the paper behind the Top and Bottom Triangle pieces.

If you are using foundation paper that needs to be completely removed, trim away the paper from the Top and Bottom Triangles only. Do not remove the rest of the paper until after it is stitched to the next block or piece. Make three more Corners in the same way.

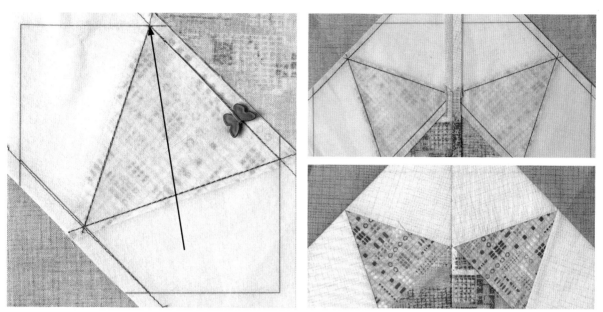

10. When piecing two Corner units together, place the pin in along the diagonal seam line, and come up at the outer seam line. Pinning in this fashion will allow you to keep the pin in while you stitch the pieces together, and the excess fabric will not "bump" away as you stitch over it (which is visible on the front). Press the seam open. Attach the other two Corner blocks to one another in the same way.

11. Following the pinning tip in step 10, pin the two halves to one another.

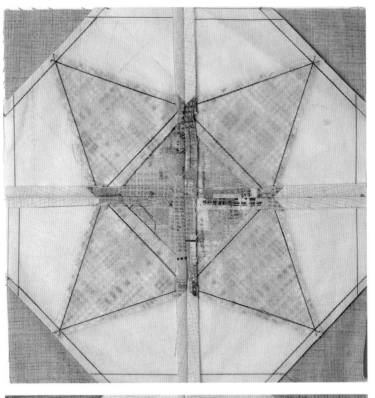

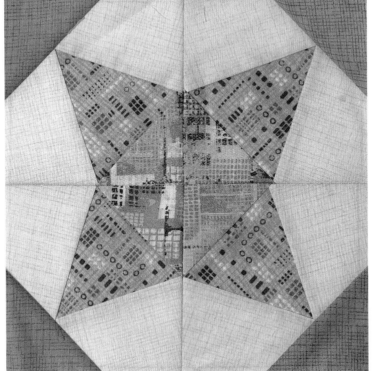

12. Sew and press the seam. The completed block will look like this.

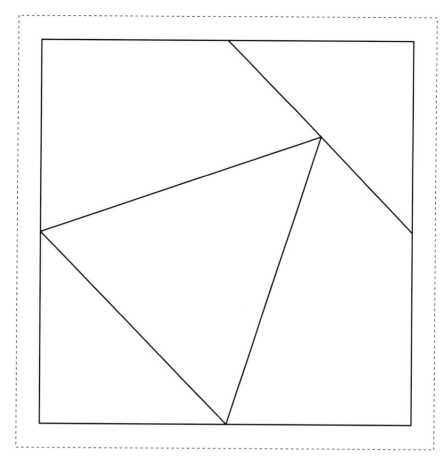

Full-size templates for Corner Triangle unit (4½" [11.45cm] unfinished)

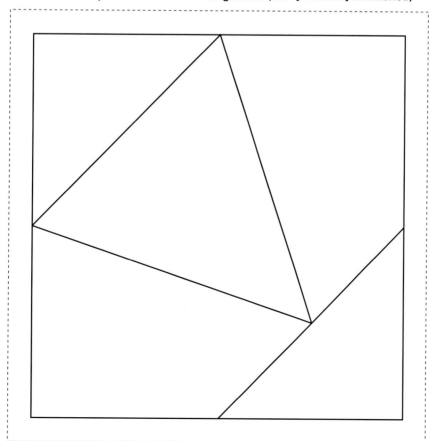

Using Connector Squares

This technique was originally made famous by the late Mary Ellen Hopkins. Depending on when you started quilting and where you reside, this technique can also be called "snowball corners," "stitch-and-flip corners," "dog-ear corners," "flippy corners," among other names. For the purposes of this book, we shall use the term *connector squares* for this technique.

You will use a smaller square (referred to as the *connector*), which is placed upon a larger square (or rectangle) that is referred to as the *base* with RST. Stitch a diagonal line from corner to corner—folding the square over onto itself diagonally—to create a triangle shape on the base fabric. Depending on what colors you are using, you will cut away one or two of the fabrics underneath this triangle corner. See the illustrations below.

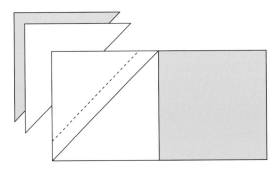

Attach a connector fabric to a base fabric by sewing on the diagonal, then cut one or both of the fabrics ABOVE the sewn line.

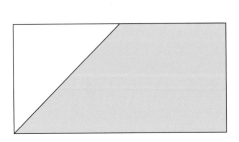

Press your seam to reveal a triangle corner.

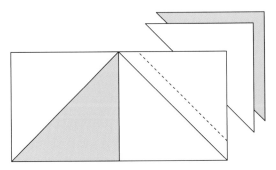

Do the same on the opposite side.

When stitching a Flying Geese unit, you must stitch, trim, and fold one side at a time. Do not add the second connector without first folding over the first.

This method is also used to create the sashing and/or border elements in London Underground (page 34) and Crown Jewels (page 57). Adding some connector squares to the border or sashing units can give you some secondary and tertiary designs in your overall quilt.

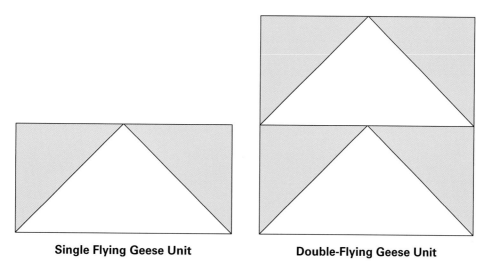

Single Flying Geese Unit   **Double-Flying Geese Unit**

Changing the angles of the connector squares will give you some additional design potential. You can now create a chevron look. It's really important that you pay attention as you stitch these units so that you have an equal amount of each, or else you may have to bust out the seam ripper and start over.

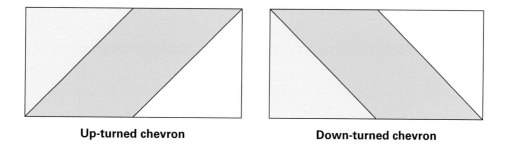

Up-turned chevron   **Down-turned chevron**

The connector square method is similarly used in making the SIS unit that we use in a few of these quilts. You will connect a square onto each corner of a larger base square to give the block a "diamond-in-a-square" look. As you stitch your SIS unit together, remember to fold and press each corner prior to adding on the next connector.

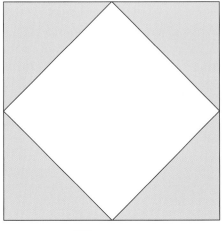

SIS connector

Half-Square Triangles

Like us, you are probably not thrilled about working with ⅛" (0.3cm) cutting increments, so we will use 3" (7.6cm) squares for this book.

The formula we use is to cut 1" (2.55cm) larger than the size of the finished HST.

Place the HST squares RST. Draw a diagonal line from corner to corner using your favorite marking tool. Stitch ¼" (0.65cm) away from that drawn line.

Cut this piece apart on the drawn line. Press the seam (usually toward the darker fabric). Trim the HST to 2½" (6.35cm). You can now use these pieces in your quilt.

When making numerous HSTs of the same colors, there are several different products on the market that will make multiple HSTs at one time. Our favorite is Triangles on a Roll. Also available are Thangles™, Triangulations™, and other products where you stitch on the paper.

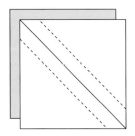

Cut along the drawn line between the two sewn lines.

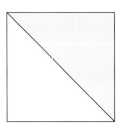

You'll end up with two identical HSTs.

Adding Borders

You have worked so hard on your blocks and are probably anxious to get the top finished so you can work on the quilting. Please do NOT rush to finish by adding the borders without measuring them. As a longarm quilter, I (Linda) have seen many beautiful quilts distorted when the borders are attached without taking the time to measure and attach them properly.

Sometimes the size of your quilt can change by the time you are ready to add the borders. This change can occur because of all the seams involved in piecework. For this reason, it is a good idea to cut the borders to the size of your actual quilt—and not necessarily to the instructions of the pattern that you are using. I always cut my borders AFTER I have pieced the inside of the top.

Size differences can also be the result of inconsistent seam allowances or pressing techniques. If at all possible, I prefer to cut my borders along the straight of grain as opposed to the cross grain. The straight of grain is parallel to the selvage edge. I will also tear the selvage off before cutting, as this edge is a much tighter weave and sometimes has printing on it.

1. Begin by starching and pressing your quilt top. Sliver-trim the sides to get them straight.

2. Measure the length of the quilt by measuring in the center, which will give you the truest measurement.

3. Cut your borders to that center measurement by the designated width of the strip.

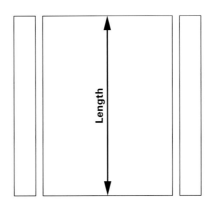
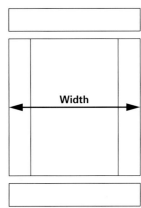

Vocabulary Lesson

WOF	Width of fabric
RST	Right sides together
RSU	Right side up
RSD	Right side down
HST	Half-Square Triangle
SIS	Square in a Square
Connector	A square stitched on the diagonal upon a larger square or rectangle and folded over to create a triangle; sometimes referred to as "snowball corners."
Seam allowance	Unless otherwise noted, a ¼" (0.64cm) seam is used throughout the projects in this book.

4. Fold both the top and the border in half—creasing the centers of each—and pin together at the creases. Pin at the top and bottom as well. If you would like more folds, you can add them.

5. If there is some excess fabric, place that side against the feed dogs so that they can help ease in the fullness. Stitch on the border without stretching the fabric.

6. Once the side borders are attached, repeat the process to attach the borders on the top and bottom of the quilt.

London Underground

We placed this quilt first because it's a very beginner-friendly project. If you're new to the Country Crown block or want to work on an easier project, start with this one. This is a five-fabric quilt that uses just the corner shape of the block. We added a little extra "zing" to the quilt using connector squares in the pieced borders.

Size: 40" x 40" (101.6 x 101.6cm)
Made and quilted by Linda J. Hahn
Fabric: Urban Grunge collection by Northcott Silk

PAPER FOUNDATION REQUIREMENTS

32 sheets (2 corner shapes per sheet), yields 64 Triangle Corner block units

FABRIC REQUIREMENTS

* ⅞ yard (0.8m) small teal print
* ⅝ yard (0.6m) teal tone on tone print
* ¾ yard (0.7m) small dark gray print
* ½ yard (0.45m) gold print
* 1½ yards (1.4m) cream print
* ½ yard (0.45m) binding fabric
* 3 yards (2.75m) backing fabric

Cutting

From the small teal print (Border), cut:

(4) 4½" (11.45cm) squares

(16) 4½" x 8½" (11.45 x 21.6cm) rectangles

From the teal tone on tone (Triangle Top and Border Connectors), cut:

(32) 3½" (8.9cm) squares for Triangle Tops, cut in half on diagonal

(36) 2½" (6.35cm) squares for Border Connectors

From the small dark gray print (Center Triangle), cut:

(64) 3½" x 4" (8.9 x 10.15cm) rectangles

From the gold print (Triangle Bottom), cut:

(32) 3½" (8.9cm) squares cut in half on the diagonal

From the cream print (Triangle Sides), cut:

(128) 3½" x 4" (8.9 x 10.15cm) rectangles

From the backing fabric, cut:

(2) 1½ yards (1.4m) cuts, seamed vertically

London Underground

Assembly

1. Following the instructions on pages 24–28, make a total of sixty-four Triangle Corner block units.

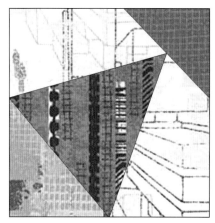

Corner Triangle Unit Assembly (make 64)

2. Assemble the Triangle block units into sixteen blocks, each containing four units.

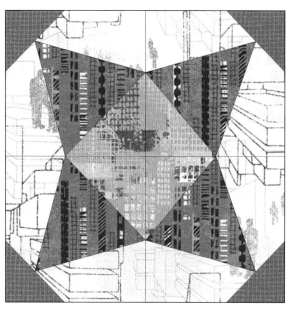

Block Assembly (make 16)

3. Stitch the quilt blocks into four rows of four blocks each. Stitch the rows into the top.

Inner Quilt Top Assembly

4. Following the instructions on page 31, stitch a 2½" (6.35cm) connector square onto one corner of a 4½" (11.45cm) border square. Make four.

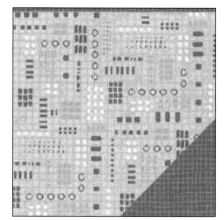

Border Square (make 4)

5. Repeat the technique to stitch a 2½" (6.35cm) connector square onto two corners of the 4½" x 8½" (11.45 x 21.6cm) border rectangle.

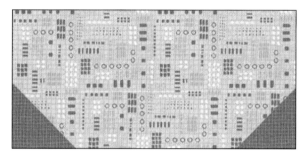

Border Rectangle Assembly (make 2)

6. Stitch together four of the border units. Make four.

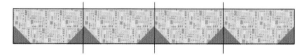

Border Strip Assembly (make 4)

7. Add a corner unit to each end of two of these border strips.

Top and Bottom Border Strip Assembly (make 2)

8. Attach the borders to the sides of the quilt, and then to the top and bottom. Give it a good press.

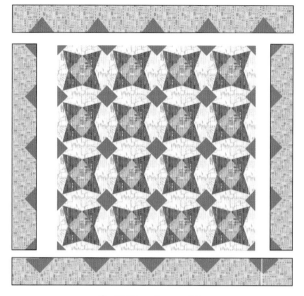

Quilt Top Assembly

9. Layer and quilt. Bind using 2½" (6.35cm) strips of your choice of fabric. Add a hanging sleeve if desired. Don't forget to add the label.

Quilt Top

Elizabethan

One thing beginner quilters might find difficult is choosing their fabrics. Get in the habit of playing with different fabric colors and prints when you're approaching a new project. Using fun floral fabric with the addition of a pieced sashing gives this quilt a completely different look. The use of the dark background gives it the illusion of curved wrought ironwork.

Size: 49" x 49" (124.45 x 124.45cm)
Made and quilted by Deborah G. Stanley
Fabric: Landscape Collection from Elizabeth's Studio

PAPER FOUNDATION REQUIREMENTS

50 sheets, yields 100 Triangle Corner block units

FABRIC REQUIREMENTS

* 2¼ yards (2.05m) dark blue fabric
* ½ yard (0.45m) purple floral print
* ⅜ yard (0.35m) blue floral print
* ¾ yard (0.7m) gold fabric (includes binding fabric)
* ¾ yard (0.7m) dark green print
* 2¼ yards (2.05m) light green print
* ½ yard (0.45m) binding fabric (see note included in gold yardage above)
* 3½ yards (3.2m) backing fabric

Cutting

From the dark blue fabric, cut:
(2) 2½" (6.35cm) x WOF strips (sashing)

(50) 3½" (8.9cm) squares cut in half on the diagonal (Triangle Top and Bottom)

(96) 3½" x 4" (8.9 x 10.15cm) rectangles (Triangle Sides)

(2) 2½" x 45½" (6.35 x 115.6cm) strips
(need to be pieced from 2½" [6.35cm] strips)

(2) 2½" x 49½" (6.35 x 125.75cm) strips
(need to be pieced from 2½" [6.35cm] strips)

From the purple floral fabric, cut:
(4) 2½" (6.35cm) x WOF strips (Sashing)

From the blue floral fabric, cut:
(2) 2½" (6.35cm) x WOF strips (Sashing)

From the gold fabric, cut:
(6) 2½" (6.35cm) x WOF strips (Binding)

(25) 1½" (3.8cm) squares (Sashing Center)

From the dark green print fabric, cut:
(52) 3½" x 4" (8.9 x 10.15cm) rectangles (Triangle Center)

From the light green print fabric, cut:
(48) 3½" x 4" (8.9 x 10.15cm) rectangles (Triangle Center)

(26) 3½" (8.9cm) squares cut in half on diagonal (Triangle Bottom)

(104) 3½" x 4" (8.9 x 10.15cm) rectangles (Triangle Sides)

From the backing fabric, cut:
(2) 1¾ yards (1.6m) cuts, seamed vertically

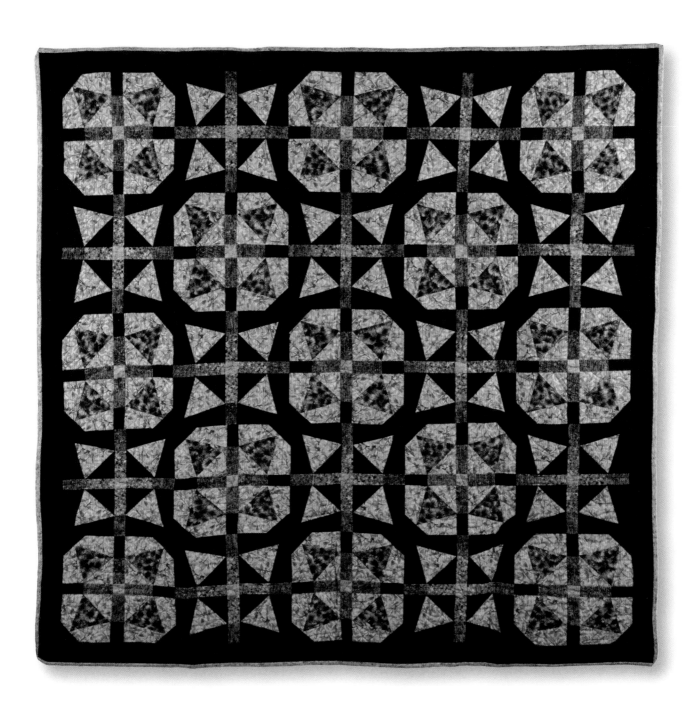

Elizabethan

Assembly

1. Following the instructions on pages 24–28, make (52) Corner units using the green print as the Triangle Center, the light green print as the Triangle Sides, and the Bottom Triangle with the dark blue as the Triangle Top.

Corner Triangle Unit A (make 52)

2. Following the instructions on pages 24–28, make (48) Corner units using the light green print as Triangle Center and the dark blue as the Triangle Sides, Triangle Top, and Triangle Bottom.

Corner Triangle Unit B (make 48)

3. Stitch together the 2½" (6.35cm) x WOF strips of the blue floral and purple floral fabric for Strip Set A. Make (2) sets.

Strip Set A (make 2)

4. Repeat for the Strip Set B using the 2½" (6.35cm) x WOF strips of the dark blue and the purple floral fabric. Make (2) sets.

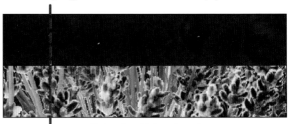

Strip Set B (make 2)

5. Cross-cut each of these strip sets into 1½" (3.8cm) segments so that you have a total of (48) of the blue floral and purple floral and (52) of the dark blue and purple floral.

6. Using half of each of the fabric combinations, stitch a 1½" (3.8cm) square of gold between them. Be sure that you are stitching the fabric in the correct placement.

Strip A (make 13)

Strip B (make 12)

7. Assemble Block A by stitching two corner units to the strip unit. Make (26). Place one of the strips with the gold center in between. Stitch together to create the block. Make (13) blocks.

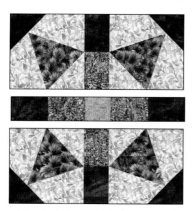

Block A Assembly (make 13)

8. Assemble Block B by repeating the steps above. Make (12) blocks.

Block Assembly B (make 12)

9. Following the diagram, stitch the blocks together into rows and then stitch the rows together to make the quilt top.

10. Please refer to the Adding Borders section on page 33. Attach a 2½" x 45½" (6.35 x 115.6cm) strip to the sides of your quilt, and a 2½" x 49½" (6.35 x 125.75cm) strip to the top and bottom of your quilt to gently frame the blocks.

Quilt Top Assembly

11. Give your quilt a good press with a hot, dry iron. Layer and baste the quilt together with the backing fabric and quilt as desired. Bind using 2½" (6.35cm) strips of the gold fabric. Add a hanging sleeve if desired. Don't forget to add the label.

Quilt Top

Afternoon Tea

In addition to the unease felt when choosing fabrics, beginner quilters may also find it a little intimidating to play with the quilt design. This quilt has the same sashed blocks as Elizabethan (page 38) but changes the background color and substitutes in some pink and purple. After rotating the blocks, you will have a completely different look to the same quilt.

> **Size: 36"x 36" (91.45 x 91.45cm)**
> **Made and quilted by Deborah G. Stanley**
> **Fabric: Toscana Collection by Northcott and Ketan Collection by Banyan Batiks**

PAPER FOUNDATION REQUIREMENTS
32 sheets to yield 64 Triangle Corner block units

FABRIC REQUIREMENTS
* 1 yard (0.9m) cream fabric
* 1 yard (0.9m) pale gray fabric
* ¾ yard (0.7m) black print fabric (includes binding fabric)
* ½ yard (0.45m) gray print fabric
* ¼ yard (0.25m) pink fabric
* ½ yard (0.45m) dark purple fabric
* ¼ yard (0.25m) light purple fabric
* ½ yard (0.45m) dark green print fabric
* ½ yard (0.45m) light green print fabric
* ⅛ yard (0.1m) gold fabric
* ⅓ yard (0.3m) dark blue print fabric
* ½ yard (0.45m) binding fabric (see note included in black yardage above)
* 1½ yards (1.4m) backing fabric

Cutting

For the cream fabric, cut:
(64) 3½" x 4" (8.9 x 10.15cm) rectangles (Triangle Sides)

For pale gray fabric, cut:
(64) 3½" x 4" (8.9 x 10.15cm) rectangles (Triangle Sides)

For black print fabric, cut:
(4) 2½" (6.35cm) x WOF strips (Sashing)

(5) 2½" (6.35cm) x WOF strips (if using black for binding)

For gray print fabric, cut:
(4) 2½" (6.35cm) x WOF strips (Sashing)

For pink fabric, cut:
(8) 3½" (8.9cm) squares cut in half on diagonal (Triangle Bottom)

For dark purple fabric, cut:
(32) 3½" (8.9cm) squares cut in half on diagonal (Triangle Tops and Bottoms)

For light purple fabric, cut:
(8) 3½" (8.9cm) squares cut in half on diagonal (Triangle Bottom)

For dark green print fabric, cut:
(32) 3½" x 4" (8.9 x 10.15cm) rectangles (Triangle Center)

For light green print fabric, cut:
(32) 3½" x 4" (8.9 x 10.15cm) rectangles (Triangle Center)

For gold fabric, cut:
(64) 1" (2.55cm) squares (Sashing)

For dark blue fabric, cut:
(16) 3½" (8.9cm) squares cut in half on diagonal (Triangle Tops)

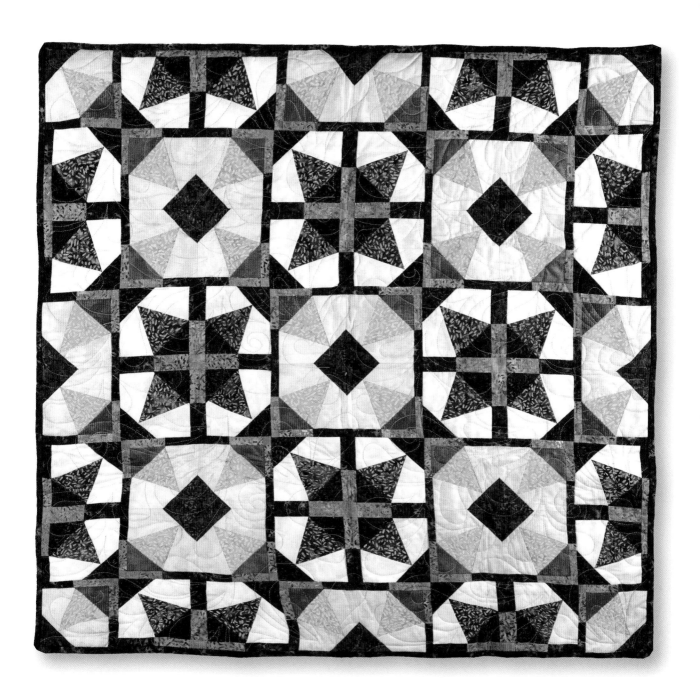

Afternoon Tea

Assembly

1. Following the instructions on pages 24–28, make the corner blocks. Make (16) using the 3½" x 4" (8.9 x 10.15cm) light green for the Triangle Center, 3½" x 4" (8.9 x 10.15cm) pale gray for the Triangle Sides, and the triangles cut on the diagonal for the light purple Triangle Bottom and the blue Triangle Top.

Corner Triangle Unit A (make 16)

2. Make (32) using the 3½" x 4" (8.9 x 10.15cm) dark green fabric for the Triangle Center, 3½" x 4" (8.9 x 10.15cm) cream for the Triangle Sides, and the triangles cut on the diagonal for the purple Triangle Bottom and Triangle Top.

Corner Triangle Unit B (make 32)

3. Make (16) using the 3½" x 4" (8.9 x 10.15cm) light green for the Triangle Center, 3½" x 4" (8.9 x 10.15cm) pale gray for the Triangle Sides, and the triangles cut on the diagonal for the pink Triangle Bottom and the blue Triangle Top.

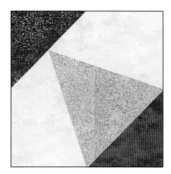

Corner Triangle Unit C (make 16)

4. Stitch together the 2½" (6.35cm) x WOF strips of the black and gray print strips. Crosscut each of these strips into 1" (2.55cm) segments for a total of (128). Stitch a 1" (2.55cm) square of gold onto the gray end of half of these cut strips. Make (64).

Strip (make 128)

Sashing Strip (make 64)

5. Add one of the black/gray units cut from the strip set to the side of each of the Corner units (make sure that the black fabric is at the top). Then add one of the black/gray/gold strips to the bottom, again making sure that the black fabric is at the top. Repeat this step for each of the Corner units.

Corner Triangle

Block A (make 16)   **Block B (make 32)**   **Block C (make 16)**

6. Referring to the image, stitch the above units into a larger block. Please lay the units out prior to stitching so that you get the correct orientation of each of the pieces. Make (16).

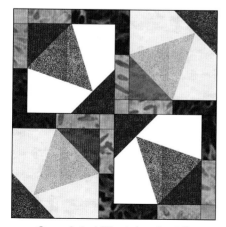

Completed Block (make 16)

7. Referring to the image, rotating the blocks around, stitch the blocks into rows and the rows into blocks. Have some fun and rotate the blocks around some more to see what happens!

Quilt Top Assembly

8. Give your quilt a good press with a hot, dry iron. Layer and baste the quilt together with the backing fabric and quilt as desired. Bind using 2½" (6.35cm) strips of the black fabric. Add a hanging sleeve if desired. Don't forget to add the label.

Quilt Top

Countryside

The original Country Crown block along with a modified version in autumn hues give this quilt a warm and cozy feeling. Always remember that you can add a solid-colored border around your quilt top. Framing your quilt like this will allow the design to take center stage.

Size: 58" x 58" (147.3 x 147.3cm)
Made by Nancy Rock (Edison, NJ); Quilted by Deborah G. Stanley
Fabric: Shadows Collection by Banyan Batiks

PAPER FOUNDATION REQUIREMENTS

32 sheets to yield 64 Triangle Corner block units

FABRIC REQUIREMENTS

✳ 2½ yards (2.3m) cream fabric

✳ ½ yard (0.45m) burgundy fabric

✳ ¾ yard (0.7m) gold fabric

✳ ⅔ yard (0.6m) orange fabric

✳ 1 yard (0.9m) blue fabric

✳ 1⅛ yards (1m) rust fabric

✳ ¼ yard (0.45m) turquoise fabric

✳ ½ yard (0.45m) dark green fabric

✳ ½ yard (0.45m) green fabric

✳ ⅛ yard (0.1m) red fabric

✳ ⅝ yard (0.6m) binding

✳ 4 yards (3.65m) backing fabric

Cutting

From the cream fabric, cut:
(32) 2½" x 4½" (6.35 x 11.45cm) rectangles (Flying Geese)

(128) 3½" x 4" (8.9 x 10.15cm) rectangles (Triangle Sides)

(32) 3½" (8.9cm) squares cut in half on diagonal (Triangle Bottoms)

(8) 4½" (11.45cm) squares (SIS)

(64) 2½" (6.35cm) squares (Connectors)

From the burgundy fabric, cut:
(32) 2½" (6.35cm) squares (SIS)

(16) 3½" (8.9cm) squares cut in half on diagonal (Triangle Tops)

From the gold fabric, cut:
(64) 2½" (6.35cm) squares (Connectors)

(6) 1½" (3.8cm) x WOF strips (Inner Border)

(4) 4½" (11.45cm) squares (Border Corners)

From the orange fabric, cut:
(1) 2½" (6.35cm) x WOF strip (Four Patch)

(32) 3½" x 4" (8.9 x 10.15cm) rectangles (Triangle Center)

From the blue fabric, cut:
(64) 2½" (6.35cm) squares (Connectors)

(64) 2½" x 4½" (6.35cm x 11.45cm) rectangles

From the rust fabric, cut:
(16) 3½" (8.9cm) squares cut in half on diagonal (Triangle Tops)

(6) 4½" (11.45cm) x WOF (Outer Border)

From the turquoise fabric, cut:
(32) 2½" x 4½" (6.35 x 11.45cm) rectangles (Flying Geese)

From the dark green fabric, cut:
(64) 2½" (6.35cm) squares (Connectors)

From the green fabric, cut:
(32) 3½" x 4" (8.9 x 10.15cm) rectangles (Triangle Centers)

From the red fabric, cut:
(1) 2½" (6.35cm) x WOF strip (Four Patch)

From the binding fabric, cut:
(7) 2½" (6.35cm) x WOF strips

From the backing fabric, cut:
(2) 2 yards (1.85m) cuts, seamed vertically

Countryside

Assembly
BLOCK 1 (MAKE 8)

1. Following the instructions on pages 24–28, make (32) Corner units using the 3½" x 4" (8.9 x 10.15cm) green rectangles for the Center Triangle, 3½" x 4" (8.9 x 10.15cm) cream for the Side Triangles, 3½" (8.9cm) cream triangles for the Triangle Bottom, and 3½" (8.9cm) burgundy triangles for the Triangle Top.

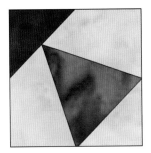

**Block 1 Corner Unit
(make 32)**

2. Stitch a 2½" (6.35cm) x WOF strip of red to the 2½" (6.35cm) strip of orange. Crosscut this strip set into (16) 2½" (6.35cm) segments. Stitch the segments into (8) Four-Patch units.

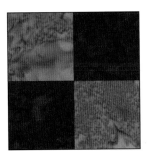

**Block 1 Four-Patch Unit
(make 8)**

3. Following the directions on page 32, connect a 2½" (6.35cm) cream square onto the 2½" x 4½" (6.35 x 11.45cm) blue rectangle. Connect a 2½" (6.35cm) gold square onto the opposite end of the blue rectangle. Make (32) of each orientation. Stich together into (32) units.

 +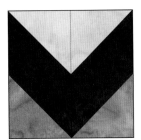

Block 1 Connector Units   **Block 1 Chevron Unit**
(make 32)   **(make 32)**

4. Referring to the Block 1 Assembly diagram, stitch the block components into rows and the rows into the block. Make (8).

**Block 1 Assembly
(make 8)**

BLOCK 2 (MAKE 8)

1. Following the instructions on pages 24–28, make (32) Corner units using the orange as Triangle Center, the cream as the Triangle Sides and Bottom Triangle, with the rust as the Triangle Top.

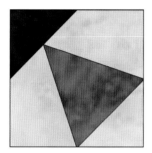

**Block 2 Corner Unit
(make 32)**

2. Following the instructions on page 31, make (32) Flying Geese units using the 2½" x 4½" (6.35 x 11.45cm) cream rectangles with 2½" (6.35cm) dark green connectors and then the 2½" x 4½" (6.35 x 11.45cm) turquoise rectangles with 2½" (6.35cm) blue connectors. Stitch the units together with the green/cream unit on top.

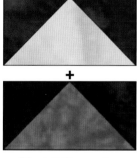
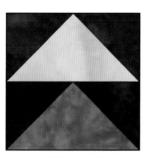

**Block 2 Connector
Units (make 32)**   **Block 2 Flying Geese
Unit (make 32)**

3. Following the instructions on page 32, make (8) SIS units using the 4½" (11.45cm) squares of cream with 2½" (6.35cm) burgundy connectors.

**Block 2 SIS Unit
(make 8)**

4. Referring to the Block 2 Assembly diagram, stitch the block components into rows and the rows into blocks. Make (8).

**Block 2 Assembly
(make 8)**

Finishing

1. Sew (4) blocks together to create a row, then sew the four rows together to create the quilt top.

2. Please refer to the Adding Borders section on page 33. Attach a 1½" x 48½" (3.8 x 123.2cm) strip to the sides of your quilt and a 1½" x 50½" (3.8 x 128.3cm) strip to the top and bottom of your quilt to gently frame the blocks.

3. Add a 4½" x 50½" (11.45 x 128.3cm) strip of rust to each side. Then add a 4½" (11.45cm) gold corner on each end of the remaining two strips of rust, and sew the strips to the top and bottom of the quilt.

4. Layer and baste your quilt top, then quilt as desired. Bind using 2½" (6.35cm) strips of binding fabric. Add a hanging sleeve if desired. Don't forget to add the label.

Quilt Top

Quilt Top Assembly

Tiara

Take note of the design in this quilt. Careful placement of the dark blue fabric creates the illusion of a secondary circle effect. Even the smallest fabric pieces in a quilt can add greatly to the design.

Size: 69" x 85" (175.25 x 215.9cm)
Made by Janet Byard (Lawrenceville, NJ); Quilted by Deborah G. Stanley
Fabric: Ketan and Shadows Collections by Banyan Batiks

PAPER FOUNDATION REQUIREMENTS

40 sheets to yield 80 Triangle Corner block units

FABRIC REQUIREMENTS

* 2 yards (1.85m) multicolor pastel batik fabric

* 2½ yards (2.3m) dark blue fabric

* 5 yards (4.6m) cream fabric

* ¾ yard (0.7m) light blue fabric

* ⅛ yard (0.1m) of (20) different pastel colors OR 2 yards (1.85m) single color fabric (we used [20] 10" [25.4cm] squares of pastel color)

* ⅔ yard (0.6m) binding fabric

* 5½ yards (5m) backing fabric

Cutting

From the multicolor pastel batik fabric, cut:
(20) 3½" (8.9cm) squares cut in half on diagonal (Triangle Tops)

(120) 2½" (6.35cm) squares (Connectors)

(2) 2" (5.1cm) x WOF strips (Sashing Four Patch)

(10) 2½" (6.35cm) x WOF strips (Border)

From the dark blue fabric, cut:
(120) 2½" x 4½" (6.35 x 11.45cm) rectangles (Flying Geese)

(40) 3½" x 4" (8.9 x 10.15cm) rectangles (Triangle Center)

(20) 3½" (10.15cm) squares cut in half on diagonal (Triangle Tops)

(2) 2" (5.1cm) x WOF strips (Four Patch Sashing)

(2) 2" x 72½" (5.1 x 184.15cm) strips (Side Borders), pieced from (4) 2" (5.1cm) strips

(2) 2½" x 60½" (6.35 x 153.7cm) strips (Top and Bottom Borders) pieced from (4) 2½" (6.35cm) strips

From the cream fabric, cut:
(160) 3½" x 4" (8.9 x 10.15cm) rectangles (Triangle Sides)

(80) 2½" (6.35cm) squares (Connectors)

(40) 3½" (8.9cm) squares cut in half on diagonal (Triangle Bottom)

(40) 2½" x 4½" (6.35 x 11.45cm) rectangles (Block 2)

(10) 4½" (11.45cm) squares (SIS Block 2)

(31) 3½" x 12½" (8.9 x 31.75cm) rectangles (Sashing)

From the light blue fabric, cut:
(20) 2½" (6.35cm) squares (Four Patch)

(80) 2½" (6.35cm) squares (Connectors)

From (10) pastel colors (for Block 1), cut from each:
(4) 3½" x 4" (8.9 x 10.15cm) rectangles (Triangle Centers)

(2) 2½" (6.35cm) squares (Four Patch)

From the remaining (10) pastel colors, cut
(8) 2½" (6.35cm) squares (Connectors)

From the binding fabric, cut:
(9) 2½" (6.35cm) x WOF strips

From the backing fabric, cut:
(2) 2¾ yards (2.5m) cuts, seamed vertically

Tiara

Assembly
BLOCK 1 (MAKE 10)

1. Following the instructions on pages 24–28, make (40) Corner units using the 3½" x 4" (8.9 x 10.15cm) pastel color rectangles for the Center Triangle, 3½" x 4" (8.9 x 10.15cm) cream for the Side Triangles, 3½" (8.9cm) cream triangles for the Triangle Bottom, and 3½" (8.9cm) multicolor pastel triangles for the Triangle Top. Make (32).

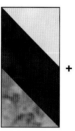

**Block 1 Triangle Corner Unit
(make 32)**

2. Stitch together (2) each of the light blue ½" (1.3cm) squares and pastel-color squares. Stitch the segments into (8) Four Patch units. Make (10).

**Four Patch Unit
(make 32)**

3. Following the directions on page 32, connect a 2½" (6.35cm) cream square onto the 2½" x 4½" (6.35 x 11.45cm) dark blue rectangle. Connect a 2½" (6.35cm) multicolor pastel square onto the opposite side of the dark blue rectangle. Make (40).

4. Repeat the process, changing the angles of the connectors on the remaining 2½" x 4½" (6.35 x 11.45cm) dark blue rectangles. Make (40).

5. Stitch the two rectangle units together for a total of (40) of each side.

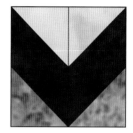 

**Block 1 Connector Units   Block 1 Chevron Unit
(make 40)   (make 40)**

6. Referring to the image, stitch the block components into rows and the rows into the block. Make (10). Keep the same Four Patch coloring the same as the corner triangles, or you can certainly mix and match in between the blocks.

**Block 1 Assembly
(make 10)**

BLOCK 2 (MAKE 10)

1. Following the instructions on pages 24–28, make (40) Corner units using the dark blue 3½" x 4" (8.9 x 10.15cm) rectangles as Triangle Center, 3½" (8.9cm) triangles for the Triangle Top, 3½" x 4" (8.9 x 10.15cm) cream rectangles as the Triangle Sides, and 3½" (8.9cm) cream triangles for the Triangle Bottom.

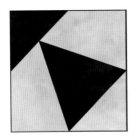

**Block 2 Triangle Corner Unit
(make 40)**

2. Following the instructions on page 31, make (40) Flying Geese units using the 2½" x 4½" (6.35 x 11.45cm) cream rectangles with 2½" (6.35cm) pastel color connectors and then the 2½" x 4½" (6.35 x 11.45cm) dark blue rectangles with 2½" (6.35cm) light blue connectors. Make (40).

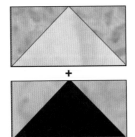
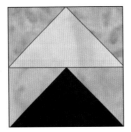

**Block 2 Flying Geese Unit
(make 40)**

3. Following the instructions on page 32, make (10) SIS units using the 4½" (11.45cm) squares of cream with 2½" (6.35cm) multicolor pastel connectors.

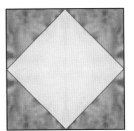

**Block 2 SIS Unit
(make 10)**

4. Stitch the block components into rows and the rows into blocks. Make (10).

**Block 2 Assembly
(make 10)**

FOUR-PATCH CORNERSTONES

1. Stitch together the 2" (5.1cm) x WOF multi-pastel batik fabric and the 2" (5.1cm) x WOF dark blue fabric strips. Make (2).

2. Crosscut these strip sets into (24) 2" (5.1cm) segments. Stitch these segments into a total of (12) Four Patch units.

**Four-Patch
Unit (make 12)**

CHECKERBOARD BORDERS

1. Stitch together the 2½" (6.35cm) x WOF multicolor pastel fabric and 2½" (6.35cm) x WOF cream strips. Make (5) sets.

2. Crosscut these strip sets into a total of (72) units.

3. Repeat this step with the 2½" (6.35cm) x WOF multicolor pastel fabric to the 2½" (6.35cm) x WOF light blue strips. Make (5) sets.

4. Crosscut these strips into a total of (72) units.

5. Referring to the Side Border illustration for color placement, stitch (38) segments together to create each of the side borders.

6. Referring to the Top and Bottom Border illustration for color placement, stitch (34) segments together to create the top and bottom borders.

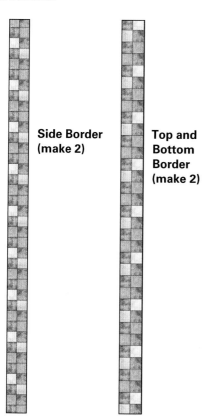

Side Border (make 2)

Top and Bottom Border (make 2)

Finishing

1. Lay out and organize the pieced blocks into rows. Stitch the rows together, inserting a 3½" x 1½" (8.9 x 3.8cm) strip of sashing in between the blocks. **Note:** When stitching the sashing strips together, make sure that you pay attention to the orientation of the Four Patch colors (some have dark blue on top left and some have dark blue on top right). Insert a Four Patch sashing row in between the block rows.

Four-Patch Sashing Row

2. Following the Sashing Row Assembly diagram, sew the rows of blocks and rows of sashing together into your quilt top.

Sashing Row Assembly

3. Please refer to the Adding Borders section on page 33. Attach a 2" x 72½" (5.1 x 184.15cm) strip of dark blue to the sides of your quilt, and a 2½" x 60½" (6.35 x 153.7cm) dark blue strip to the top and bottom of your quilt. (**Note:** the width of the side border strips is different than the top and bottom border strips.)

4. Add the checkerboard border with (38) segments to the sides of the quilt, and then the checkerboard border with the (34) segments to the top and bottom of the quilt. See the Quilt Top Assembly diagram for reference.

5. Give your quilt top a good press. Layer, baste, and quilt as desired. Bind using the 2½" (6.35cm) x WOF strips of dark blue. Add a hanging sleeve if desired. Don't forget to add the label.

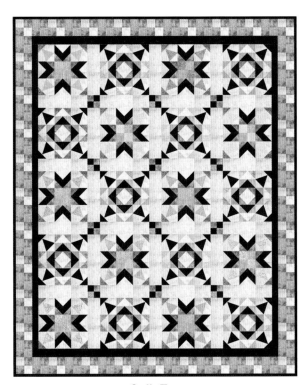

Quilt Top

Quilt Top Assembly

Crown Jewels

Linda's husband, Allan, made this and it's his very first quilt! Starting out with this quilt was a challenge, but it turned out beautifully in the end. We added a SIS for the sashing corners and then put some connectors on the sashing strips to add a secondary star pattern, which we carried out into the border.

Size: 60" x 76" (152.4 x 193.05cm)
Made by Allan W. Hahn (Palm Bay, FL); Quilted by Linda J. Hahn
Fabric: Timeless Treasures

PAPER FOUNDATION REQUIREMENTS

24 sheets to yield 48 Triangle Corner block units

FABRIC REQUIREMENTS

The following fabrics are the "constant" throughout this quilt

✳ 4½ yards (4.1m) cream fabric

✳ ¼ yard (0.25m) blue #1 fabric

✳ ¼ yard (0.25m) blue #2 fabric

✳ ¼ yard (0.25m) burgundy fabric

✳ ¼ yard (0.25m) light gray fabric

✳ ½ yard (0.45m) red fabric

✳ 1⅛ yards (1.05m) black fabric (includes binding fabric)

✳ 3½ yards (2.3m) assorted color fabric

✳ 5 yards (4.6m) backing fabric

Cutting

From the cream fabric, cut:

(96) 2½" (6.35cm) squares (Flying Geese Connectors)

(96) 3½" x 4" (8.9 x 10.15cm) (Triangle Sides)

(20) 4½" (11.45cm) squares (SIS Centers, Borders)

(45) 4½" x 12½" (11.45 x 31.75cm) rectangles (Borders and Sashing)

(4) 8½" (21.6cm) squares (Border Corner)

From the blue #1 fabric, cut:

(20) 2½" (6.35cm) squares (Connectors)

From the blue #2 fabric, cut:

(20) 2½" (6.35cm) squares (Connectors)

From the burgundy fabric, cut:

(24) 2½" (6.35cm) squares (Connectors)

From the light gray fabric, cut:

(6) 4½" (11.45cm) squares (SIS Center)

From the red fabric, cut:

(24) 3½" (8.9cm) squares cut in half on diagonal (Triangle Tops)

From the black fabric, cut:

(124) 2½" (6.35cm) squares (Connectors)

(6) 2½" (6.35cm) x WOF strips (Binding)

From the assorted color fabrics, you will be making (12) Blocks; cut as follows:

(12) sets of (4) 3½" x 4" (8.9 x 10.15cm) rectangles (Triangle Centers)

(12) sets of (8) 2½" x 4½" (6.35 x 11.45cm) rectangles (Flying Geese)

(12) sets of (8) 2½" (6.35cm) squares (Connectors)

(24) pairs 2½" (6.35cm) squares (Four Patch)

(24) pairs 3½" (8.9cm) squares cut in half on diagonal (Triangle Bottom)

From the backing fabric, cut:

(2) 2½ yards (2.3m) cuts, seamed vertically

Crown Jewels

Assembly

BLOCK CONSTRUCTION (MAKE 12)

1. You will need the following from the "constant" colors in each of the blocks.
- (96) cream 2½" (6.35cm) squares (Connectors)
- (96) cream 3½" x 4" (8.9 x 10.15cm) rectangles (Triangle Sides)
- (24) red 3½" (8.9cm) squares cut in half on the diagonal

2. For each block, you will then need an assortment of colors.

Ⓐ (1) set of (8) 2½" x 4½" (6.35 x 11.45cm) rectangles

Ⓑ (1) set of (4) 3½" x 4" (8.9 x 10.15cm) rectangles (Triangle Center)

Ⓒ (1) set of (8) 2½" (6.35cm) squares (Connectors)

Ⓓ (1) set of (4) triangles cut from (2) 3½" (8.9cm) squares cut in half on diagonal (Triangle Bottoms)

Ⓔ (1) set of (2) 2½" (6.35cm) squares (Four Patch)

Ⓕ (1) set of (2) 2½" (6.35cm) squares (Four Patch)

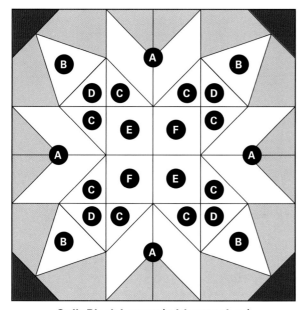

Quilt Block Layout (without colors)

3. Following the instructions on pages 24–28 and the Triangle Corner unit illustration, stitch together sets of (4) Corner block units using identical Triangle Center and Triangle bottom colors. Each of the blocks should have cream side units and a red triangle top (cut from the 3½" [8.9cm] red squares).

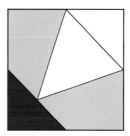

Triangle Corner Unit

4. Following the instructions on page 32 and the Flying Geese unit illustration, stitch together sets of (4) Flying Geese units using the 2½" (6.35cm) squares of cream as the top connectors.

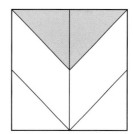

Flying Geese Unit

5. Choose two sets of (2) 2½" (6.35cm) squares and stitch them into a Four-Patch unit.

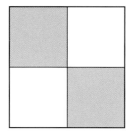

Four-Patch Unit

SQUARE IN A SQUARE

1. Follow the instructions on page 32 and the SIS Unit A diagram. Make (10) SIS Unit A's using the 4½" (11.45cm) cream square with half blue 2½" (6.35cm) square connectors and half dark blue 2½" (6.35cm) square connectors.

SIS Unit A (make 10)

2. Follow the instructions on page 32 and the SIS Unit B diagram. Make (6) SIS Unit B's using the 4½" (11.45cm) light gray square with burgundy 2½" (6.35cm) square connectors.

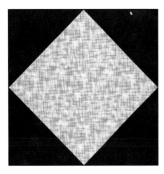

SIS Unit B (make 6)

SASHING BETWEEN THE BLOCKS

1. Follow the instructions on page 32 for all sashing units in this section. For this step, refer to the Sashing Unit A diagram. Make (23) using the 4½" x 12½" (11.45 x 31.75cm) cream rectangles with 2½" (6.35cm) black square connectors.

Sashing Unit A (make 23)

2. Refer to the Sashing Unit B diagram for this step. Make (10) using the 4½" (11.45cm) Cream square with 2½" (6.35cm) black square connectors.

Sashing Unit B (make 10)

3. Refer to the Sashing Unit C diagram for this step. Make (8) using the 4½" x 12½" (11.45 x 31.75cm) cream rectangles and 2½" (6.35cm) black square connectors.

Sashing Unit C (make 8)

Finishing

1. To make the top and bottom rows, refer to the Top and Bottom Rows diagram for placement. Stitch the two border rows together, then add an 8½" (21.6cm) square of cream to each end.

Top and Bottom Rows (make 2)

Make (2).

2. Referring to the Quilt Top Assembly diagram, stitch the blocks into rows, inserting a pieced sashing unit in between. Add a pieced sashing unit and the solid 12½" (31.75cm) cream rectangle to the ends of the row. Add one of the border units (you just made in the last step) to the top and one to the bottom of the quilt top.

3. Give your top a good final press and then layer and baste for quilting. Quilt as desired. Bind using the 2½" (6.35cm) x WOF strips for binding. Add a hanging sleeve if desired. Don't forget to add the label.

Quilt Top Assembly

Quilt Top

Bangers and Mash

Rearranging the design elements in the quilt will give your project extra interest and a unique design. The addition of multicolor Flying Geese sashing and SIS cornerstones creates secondary and tertiary patterns within this bright, happy quilt.

> **Size: 52" x 52" (132.1 x 132.1cm)**
> **Made by Sharon Dow (Palm Bay, FL); Quilted by Linda J. Hahn**
> **Fabric: 1895 Collection by Hoffman California**

PAPER FOUNDATION REQUIREMENTS

32 sheets to yield 64 Triangle Corner block units

FABRIC REQUIREMENTS

* 3½ yards (3.2m) white background fabric
* ½ yard (0.45m) bright green fabric
* ½ yard (0.45m) soft green fabric
* ½ yard (0.45m) red fabric
* ½ yard (0.45m) purple fabric
* ½ yard (0.45m) hot pink fabric
* ½ yard (0.45m) orange fabric
* ½ yard (0.45m) bright coral fabric
* 1 yard (0.9m) green fabric
* ½ yard (0.45m) binding fabric
* 3½ yards (3.2m) backing fabric

Cutting

From the white fabric, cut:

(25) 4½" (11.45cm) squares (Square in Square)

(128) 3½" x 4" (8.9 x 10.15cm) rectangles (Triangle Sides)

(320) 2½" (6.35cm) squares (Flying Geese)

From the bright green fabric, cut:
(32) 3½" x 4" (8.9 x 10.15cm) rectangles (Triangles)

From the soft green fabric, cut:
(32) 3½" x 4" (8.9 x 10.15cm) rectangles (Triangles)

From the red fabric, cut:
(32) 3½" (8.9cm) squares cut in half on diagonal (Triangle Bottom)

From the purple, hot pink, orange, and bright coral fabrics, cut:
(40) 2½" x 4½" (6.35 x 11.45cm) rectangles from each color (Flying Geese)

From the green fabric, cut:
(32) 3½" (8.9cm) squares cut in half on diagonal (Triangle Top)

(100) 2½" (6.35cm) squares (Square in Square connectors)

From the backing fabric, cut:
(2) 1¾ yards (4.45m) cuts, seamed vertically

Bangers and Mash

Assembly

1. Following the instructions on page 32, make (25) SIS units using the 4½" (11.45cm) squares of white and the 2½" (6.35cm) squares of green as connectors.

SIS Unit (make 25)

2. Following the instructions on page 31, make (40) Flying Geese units of each color with the 2½" x 4½" (6.35 x 11.45cm) rectangles of the purple, bright pink, orange, and bright coral, and the 2½" (6.35cm) squares of white for connectors. Stitch together following the image below.

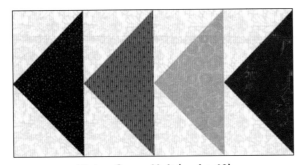

Flying Geese Unit (make 40)

3. Following the instructions on pages 24–28, make (32) Triangle Corner units from each colorway. Stitch together (4) of each unit to make a total of (8) blocks from each colorway.

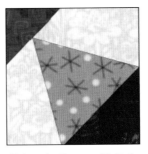 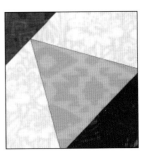

Triangle Corner Unit A
(make 32)

Triangle Corner Unit B
(make 32)

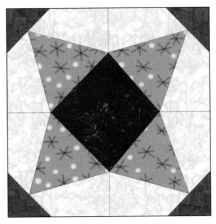

Block Unit A (make 8)

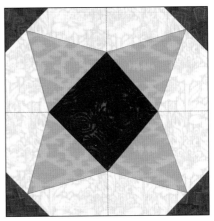

Block Unit B (make 8)

4. Referring to the image, lay out the units on your floor or design wall before you begin sewing the rows together. Please take careful note of the direction of the Flying Geese blocks. Stitch the blocks into rows and the rows into the quilt top. If you want to make this design larger, you can add some borders or more blocks.

5. Once all the rows are together, give your quilt a good press (starch if you like). Layer and baste your quilt with the batting and backing. Quilt as desired. Bind using 2½" (6.35cm) x WOF strips of the fabric of your choice. Add a hanging sleeve if desired. Don't forget to add the label.

Quilt Top Assembly

Quilt Top

Now that your quilt is together, do you see the secondary and tertiary designs that form in the quilt?

Kensington

Try different things with your quilt design, like we did here. We rotated the blocks to form a medallion at the center, then inserted some bright colors for a lively feel.

Size: 48" x 48" (121.9 x 121.9 cm)
Made and quilted by Linda J. Hahn
Fabric: 1895 Batik collection by Hoffman California

PAPER FOUNDATION REQUIREMENTS

32 sheets to yield 64 Triangle Corner block units (2 corner shapes per sheet)

FABRIC REQUIREMENTS

✳ 3 yards (2.75m) white fabric

✳ ¾ yard (0.7m) orange fabric

✳ ¾ yard (0.7m) blue fabric

✳ ⅝ yard (0.6m) green fabric

✳ ½ yard (0.45m) gold #1 fabric

✳ ⅛ yard (0.1m) (or scraps) gold #2 fabric

✳ ½ yard (0.45m) pink fabric

✳ ½ yard (.045m) purple fabric

✳ ½ yard (0.45m) binding

✳ 3 ½ yards (3.2m) backing fabric

Cutting

From white fabric, cut:
(72) 2½" (6.35cm) squares (solid squares)

(52) 3½" (8.9cm) squares cut in half on diagonal (Triangle Tops/Bottoms)

(128) 3½" x 4" (8.9 x 10.15cm) rectangles (Triangle Sides)

(108) 3" (7.6cm) squares (HST)

From the orange fabric, cut:
(16) 3" (7.6cm) squares (HST)

(12) 3½" x 4" (8.9 x 10.15cm) (Triangle Center)

(4) 3½" (8.9cm) squares cut in half on diagonal (Triangle Top)

From the blue fabric, cut:
(16) 3" (7.6cm) squares (HST)

(16) 3½" x 4" (8.9 x 10.15cm) rectangle (Triangle Center)

(6) 3½" (8.9cm) squares cut in half on diagonal (Triangle Top)

From the green fabric, cut:
(44) 3" (7.6cm) squares (HST)

(2) 3½" (8.9cm) squares cut in half on diagonal (Triangle Top)

From the gold #1 fabric, cut:
(16) 3" (7.6cm) squares (HST)

(8) 3½" x 4" (8.9 x 10.15cm) (Triangle Center)

From the gold #2/scrap fabric, cut:
(2) 3" (7.6cm) squares (HST)

From the pink fabric, cut:
(16) 3" (7.6cm) squares (HST)

(12) 3½" x 4" (8.9 x 10.15cm) (Triangle Center)

From the purple fabric, cut:
(22) 3" (7.6cm) squares (HST)

(16) 3½" x 4" (8.9 x 10.15cm) (Triangle Center)

From the binding fabric, cut:
(6) 2½" (6.35cm) x WOF strips

From the backing fabric, cut:
(2) 1¾ yards (1.6m) cuts, seamed vertically

Kensington

Assembly
BLOCK 1 (MAKE 4)

1. Following the instructions on page 32, make the following combinations using the 3" (7.6cm) squares of the designated colors.
- Make (4) pairs to yield (8) Orange/White HSTs.
- Make (8) pairs to yield (16) Blue/White HSTs.
- Make (4) pairs to yield (8) Yellow/White HSTs.
- Make (2) pairs to yield (4) Gold/Yellow HSTs.

2. Following the instructions on pages 24–28, make the following corner unit combinations. The color triangle centers should be made from 3½" x 4" (8.9 x 10.15cm) rectangles of gold #1, orange, and blue fabrics. The white side triangles should be 3½" x 4" (8.9 x 10.15cm) rectangles. The top and bottom triangles are made from 3½" (8.9cm) squares of white fabric cut in half diagonally. Make (4) Gold Triangle Centers, (4) Orange Triangle Centers, and (8) Blue Triangle Centers (see below).

Orange/White HST (make 4 pairs)

Blue/White HST (make 8 pairs)

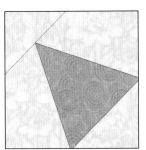
Gold Triangle Center (make 4)

Yellow/White HST (make 4 pairs)

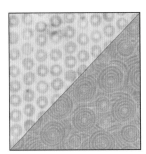
Gold/Yellow HST (make 2 pairs)

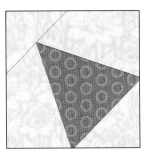
Orange Triangle Center (make 4)

Remember that each pair of squares makes two HSTs.

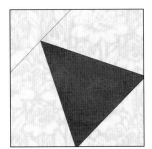
Blue Triangle Center (make 8)

3. For the solid squares in this section, you will need (44) 2½" (6.35cm) squares of white fabric. To complete the Gold Triangle Center Square, use the yellow-and-gold HSTs made in step 1 (make 4). For the Orange and Blue Triangle Center Squares, use a white square. Make (4) Orange Triangle Center Squares and (8) Blue Triangle Center Squares. See the diagrams below.

  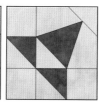

Gold Triangle Center Square (make 4) **Orange Triangle Center Square (make 4)** **Blue Triangle Center Square (make 8)**

4. Assemble the block components into the larger unit. Make (4).

Block 1 Unit (make 4)

BLOCK 2 (MAKE 8)

1. Following the instructions on page 32, make the following combinations using the 3" (7.62cm) squares of the designated colors.

- Make (16) pairs to yield (32) Purple/White HSTs.
- Make (8) pairs to yield (16) Orange/White HSTs.
- Make (44) pairs to yield (88) Green/White HSTs.

Purple/White HST (make 16 pairs)

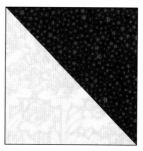

Orange/White HST (make 8 pairs)

Green/White HST (make 44 pairs)

2. Following the instructions on pages 24–28, make the following corner unit combinations. The color triangle centers should be made from 3½" x 4" (8.9 x 10.15cm) rectangles of purple, pink, and orange fabrics. The white side triangles are created from 3½" x 4" (8.9 x 10.15cm) rectangles. The top and bottom triangles are made from 3½" (8.9cm) squares of white fabric cut in half diagonally. You will also need (4) 3½" (8.9cm) blue fabric cut in half diagonally. Make (16) Purple Triangle Centers, (8) Pink Triangle Centers, and (8) Orange Triangle Centers (see below).

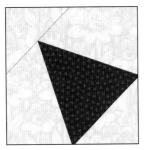

**Purple Triangle Center
(make 16)**

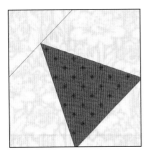

**Pink Triangle Center
(make 8)**

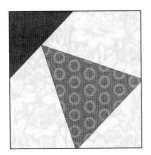

**Orange Triangle Center
(make 8)**

3. For the solid squares in this section, you will need (24) 2½" (6.35cm) squares of white fabric and the HSTs made in step 1 of this section. Make (8) Orange Triangle Center Squares, (8) Pink Triangle Center Squares, and (16) Purple Triangle Center Squares. See the diagrams below.

 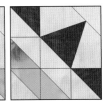

| **Orange Triangle Center Square (make 8)** | **Pink Triangle Center Square (make 8)** | **Purple Triangle Center Square (make 16)** |

4. Assemble the block components into the larger unit. Make (8).

Block 2 Unit (make 8)

BLOCK 3 (MAKE 4)

1. Following the instructions on page 32, make the following combinations using the 3" (7.6cm) squares of the designated colors.
- Make (4) pairs to yield (8) Orange/White HSTs.
- Make (8) pairs to yield (16) Blue/White HSTs.
- Make (8) pairs to yield (16) Pink/White HSTs.
- Make (4) pairs to yield (8) Pink/Gold HSTs.
- Make (2) pairs to yield (4) Purple/Gold HSTs.
- Make (4) pairs to yield (8) Pink/Purple HSTs.
- Make (4) pairs to yield (8) White/Gold HSTs.

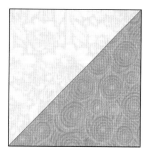

White/Gold HST (make 4 pairs)

**Orange/White HST
(make 4 pairs)**

**Blue/White HST
(make 8 pairs)**

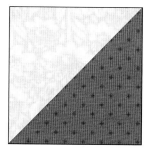

**Pink/White HST
(make 8 pairs)**

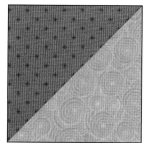

**Pink/Gold HST
(make 4 pairs)**

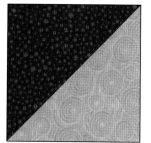

**Purple/Gold HST
(make 2 pairs)**

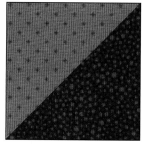

**Pink/Purple HST
(make 4 pairs)**

2. Following the instructions on pages 24–28, make the following corner unit combinations. The color triangle centers should be made from 3½" x 4" (8.9 x 10.15cm) rectangles of pink, blue, and gold fabric. The white side triangles are created from 3½" x 4" (8.9 x 10.15cm) rectangles. The bottom triangles are made from 3½" (8.9cm) squares of white fabric cut in half diagonally. You will also need (2) blue, (2) green, and (4) orange 3½" (8.9cm) squares cut in half diagonally. Make (4) Pink Triangle Centers, (4) Gold Triangle Centers, and (8) Blue Triangle Centers (see below).

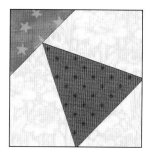

**Pink Triangle Center
(make 4)**

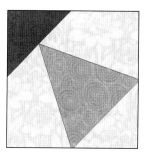

**Gold Triangle Center
(make 4)**

**Blue Triangle Center
(make 8)**

3. For the solid squares in this section, you will need (4) 2½" (6.35cm) squares of white fabric and the HSTs made in step 1 of this section. Make (4) Pink Triangle Center Squares, (4) Blue Triangle Center Squares, (4) Blue Reversed Triangle Center Squares, and (4) Gold Triangle Center Squares. See the diagrams below.

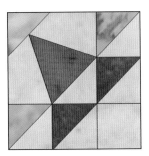

Pink Triangle Center Square (make 4)

Blue Triangle Center Square (make 4)

Blue Reversed Triangle Center Square (make 4)

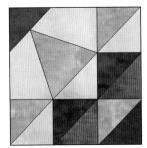

Gold Triangle Center Square (make 4)

4. Assemble the block components into the larger unit. Make (4).

Block 3 Unit (make 4)

Finishing

1. This quilt is assembled in four identical sections. Each of these four sections is further divided into four smaller sections. See the Quilt Block Assembly below.

Quilt Block Assembly

2. Stitch the (4) sections together to form the quilt top (see the Quilt Top Assembly below). If you choose, you can add borders to make this quilt a little larger.

3. Give the top a good press. Layer and quilt as desired. Bind using 2½" (6.35cm) strips of your chosen fabric. Add a hanging sleeve if desired. Don't forget to add the label.

Quilt Top Assembly

Quilt Top

Balmoral

Sometimes a simple rotation can alter the look of the entire design. If you like a certain element from a previous project but want a different look, play with the design. We rotated the blocks around from the previous quilt, which changes the whole flavor.

Size: 48" x 48" (121.9 x 121.9cm)
Made and quilted by Linda J. Hahn
Fabric: Timeless Treasures

PAPER FOUNDATION REQUIREMENTS
32 sheets to yield 64 Triangle Corner block units

FABRIC REQUIREMENTS
* 3 yards (2.75m) white fabric
* ⅝ yard (0.6m) orange fabric
* ⅛ yard (0.1m) gold fabric
* ⅜ yard (0.35m) red fabric
* ⅛ yard (0.1m) blue fabric
* ½ yard (0.45m) magenta fabric
* ½ yard (0.45m) green fabric
* ⅞ yard (0.8m) purple fabric
* ½ yard (0.45m) binding fabric
* 3½ yards (3.2m) backing fabric

Cutting

From the white fabric, cut:
(154) 3" (7.6cm) squares (HST)

(32) 3½" (8.9cm) squares cut in half on diagonal (Triangle Bottoms)

(128) 3½" x 4" (8.9 x 10.15cm) rectangles (Triangle Sides)

(12) 2½" (6.35cm) squares

From the orange fabric, cut:
(28) 3½" x 4" (8.9 x 10.15cm) rectangles (Triangle Center)

(16) 3" (7.6cm) squares (HST)

From the gold fabric, cut:
(4) 3½" x 4" (8.9 x 10.15cm) rectangles (Triangle Center)

From the red fabric, cut:
(20) 3" (7.6cm) squares (HST)

(10) 3½" (8.9cm) squares cut in half on diagonal (Triangle Top)

From the blue fabric, cut:
(12) 3" (7.6cm) squares (HST)

From the magenta fabric, cut:
(24) 3" (7.6cm) squares

(16) 3½" (8.9cm) squares cut in half on diagonal (Triangle Top)

From the green fabric, cut:
(54) 3" (7.6cm) squares (HST)

From the purple fabric, cut:
(32) 3" (7.6cm) squares (HST)

(32) 3½" x 4" (8.9 x 10.15cm) rectangles (Triangle Centers)

(6) 3½" (8.9cm) squares cut in half on diagonal

From the binding fabric, cut:
(6) 2½" (6.35cm) x WOF strips

From the backing fabric, cut:
(2) 1¾ yards (1.6m) cuts, seamed vertically

Balmoral

Assembly

BLOCK 1 (MAKE 12)

1. Following the instructions on page 32, make the following combinations using the 3" (7.6cm) squares of the designated colors.

- Make (12) pairs to yield (24) Orange/White HSTs.
- Make (12) pairs to yield (24) Red/White HSTs.
- Make (18) pairs to yield (36) Pink/White HSTs.
- Make (54) pairs to yield (108) Green/White HSTs.
- Make (24) pairs to yield (48) Purple/White HSTs.

**Orange/White HST
(make 12 pairs)**

**Red/White HST
(make 12 pairs)**

**Pink/White HST
(make 18 pairs)**

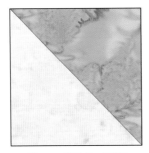

**Green/White HST
(make 54 pairs)**

**Purple/White HST
(make 24 pairs)**

> Remember that each pair of squares makes two HSTs.

2. Following the instructions on pages 24–28, make the following Triangle Corner units.

- Make (12) using the Orange Triangle Center/Purple Triangle Top and the White Triangle Bottom.
- Make (12) using the Orange Triangle Center/Red Triangle Top and White Triangle Bottom.
- Make (24) using the Purple Triangle Center/Magenta Triangle Top and White Triangle Bottom.

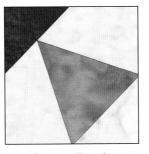

**Orange/Purple
(make 12)**

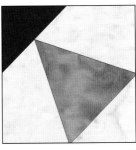

**Orange/Red
(make 12)**

**Purple/Pink
(make 24)**

3. Referring to the below diagrams, assemble the block components as indicated.

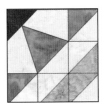

**Orange/
Purple/Green
(make 12)**

**Purple/
Pink/Green
(make 24)**

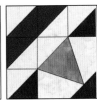

**Orange/
Red/Pink
(make 12)**

4. Stitch these blocks together into the larger block unit (make 12).

Block 1 Unit (make 12)

BLOCK 2 (MAKE 4)

1. Following the instructions on page 32, make the following combinations using the 3" (7.6cm) squares of the designated colors.
- Make (4) pairs to yield (8) Red/White HSTs.
- Make (6) pairs to yield (12) Magenta/White HSTs.
- Make (8) pairs to yield (16) Purple/White HSTs.
- Make (8) pairs to yield (16) Blue/White HSTs.
- Make (4) pairs to yield (8) Blue/Red HSTs.
- Make (4) pairs to yield (8) Orange/White HSTs.

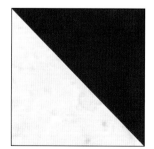 

Red/White HST (make 4 pairs) **Magenta/White HST (make 6 pairs)**

Purple/White HST (make 8 pairs) **Blue/White HST (make 8 pairs)**

Blue/Red HST (make 4 pairs) **Orange/White HST (make 4 pairs)**

2. Following the instructions on pages 24–28, make the following Triangle Corner units.
- Make (4) using the Orange Triangle Center/Red Triangle Top and the White Triangle Bottom.
- Make (8) using the Purple Triangle Center/Magenta Triangle Top and White Triangle Bottom.
- Make (4) using the Gold Triangle Center/Red Triangle Top and White Triangle Bottom.

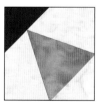 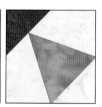

Orange/Red (make 4) **Purple/Pink (make 8)** **Gold/Red (make 4)**

3. Referring to the below diagrams, assemble the block components, inserting 2½" (6.35cm) squares of white where indicated.

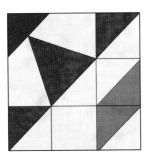

Purple/Pink/Blue Triangle Center Square
(make 4)

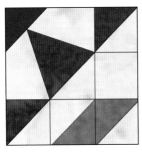

Purple/Pink/Blue Reversed Triangle Center Square
(make 4)

Orange/Red/Pink Triangle Center Square
(make 4)

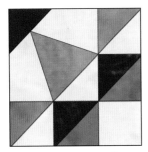

Orange/Red/Blue Triangle Center Square
(make 4)

4. Stitch these blocks together into the larger block unit (make 12).

Block 2 Unit (make 4)

5. Referring to the Quilt Top Assembly diagram, assemble the quilt top.

Quilt Top Assembly

6. Give your top a good press with a dry iron. Layer and baste together, then quilt as desired. Bind using 2½" (6.35cm) strips of your chosen binding fabric. Add a hanging sleeve if desired. Don't forget to add the label.

Quilt Top

Windsor

The easiest way to modernize a quilt design is to simplify your fabric choices. Use solid fabrics instead of patterned ones. We used a rainbow of solid colors for a modern flair in this quilt.

Size: 48" x 60" (121.9 x 152.4cm)
Made and quilted by Deborah G. Stanley
Fabric: solid fabrics

PAPER FOUNDATION REQUIREMENTS

30 sheets to yield 60 Triangle Corner block units

FABRIC REQUIREMENTS

* 2¼ yards (2.05m) white fabric
* ⅝ yard (0.6m) black fabric
* 2⅛ yards (1.95m) gray fabric
* ⅛ yard (0.1m) or 10" (25.4cm) squares of (20) different colors each
* ½ yard (0.45m) binding fabric
* 4 yards (3.65m) backing fabric

Cutting

From the white fabric, cut:

(180) 2½" (6.35cm) squares

(40) 3" (7.6cm) squares (HST)

(30) 3½" (8.9cm) squares cut in half on diagonal (Triangle Bottom)

(40) 3½" x 4" (8.9 x 10.15cm) rectangles (Triangle Sides)

(5) 3½" (8.9cm) squares cut in half on diagonal (Triangle Top)

From the black fabric, cut:

(20) 3½" x 4" (8.9 x 10.15cm) rectangles (Triangle Center)

(5) 3½" (8.9cm) squares cut in half on diagonal (Triangle Top)

(20) 3" (7.6cm) squares (HST)

From the gray fabric, cut:

(20) 6½" (16.5cm) squares

(80) 3½" x 4" (8.9 x 10.15cm) rectangles (Triangle Sides)

(20) 3½" (8.9cm) squares cut in half on diagonal (Triangle Top)

From each of the colored fabrics, cut:

(2) 3½" x 4" (8.9 x 10.15cm) rectangles (Triangle Centers)

(2) 3" (7.6cm) squares (HST)

(1) 2½" (6.35cm) square (Connector)

From the binding fabric, cut:

(6) 2½" (6.35cm) x WOF strips

From the backing fabric, cut:

(2) 2 yards (1.85m), seamed vertically

Windsor

Assembly

1. This block is constructed a bit differently from the other ones so that you have a nice big space to showcase free-motion quilting.

2. Follow the instructions on pages 24–28 to make the black/white corner units, and the instructions on page 32 for the HST units.
- Make (10) corner units using the 3½" x 4" (8.9 x 10.15cm) black rectangle for the Triangle Center and a black triangle cut from the 3½" (8.9cm) squares for the Triangle Top. (See Black/White/Black Triangle Corner Unit below.)

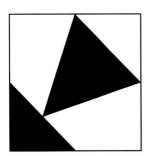

Black/White/Black Triangle Corner Unit
(make 10)

- Make (10) corner units using the 3½" x 4" (8.9 x 10.15cm) black rectangle for the Triangle Center and a triangle cut from the 3½" (8.9cm) square for the Triangle Top and Triangle Bottom. (See Black/White Triangle Corner Unit below.)

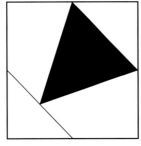

Black/White Triangle Corner Unit
(make 10)

- Make (40) HSTs from the 3" (7.6cm) squares of black and white. (See Black/White HST below.)

Black/White HST
(make 20 pairs)

3. Once again refer to the instructions on pages 24–28 for the corner unit construction, and page 32 for the HST construction. You will make (2) HSTs of white and a color to yield (4) HSTs of the color and white. Use the 3½" x 4" (8.9 x 10.15cm) rectangle of the same color you just used and the gray fabric to make the corner unit.
- Make (2) using the 3½" x 4" (8.9 x 10.15cm) rectangles of a color for the Triangle Center, the 3½" x 4" (8.9 x 10.15cm) gray rectangles for the Triangle Sides, a gray triangle cut from the 3½" (8.9cm) gray squares for the Triangle Top, and a white triangle cut from the 3½" (8.9cm) white square for the Triangle Bottom. (See Red/Gray Triangle Corner unit below.)

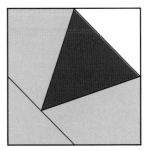

Red/Gray Triangle Corner Unit
(make 2)

- Make (4) HSTs from each of the 3" (7.6cm) color squares and 3" (7.6cm) white squares. (See Red/Gray HST below.)

Red/White HST
(make 2 pairs)

4. Referring to the Black/White/Black unit diagram below, assemble the black and white units with the Black/White/Black Triangle Corner unit (from step 2) into the block, adding in the 2½" (6.35cm) squares of white. Make sure that each of the block units is oriented correctly. Make (10).

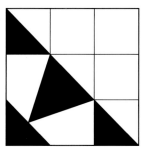

Black/White/Black Unit
(make 10)

5. Referring to the image, repeat the process for the black and white units (made using the Black/White Triangle Corner units from step 2), adding in the 2½" (6.35cm) squares of white. Make sure that each of the blocks is oriented correctly. Make (10).

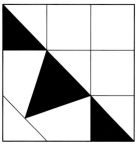

Black/White/Black Unit
(make 10)

6. Referring to the image, assemble the Gray/Color/White units into the block adding in the 2½" (6.35cm) white squares. Make sure that each of the blocks is oriented correctly. Make (2) from each of the (20) colors.

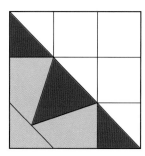

Gray/Color/White Unit
(make 2)

7. Now it is time to lay out your blocks on a design wall or the floor to make a determination of how you wish your colors to flow. It is VITALLY important to do this before you begin to stitch these blocks into larger units. It keeps the colors flowing fluidly and creates the zigzag look. There are two things that you need to take note of as you lay out the design. The corner units with the **white Triangle Top** go through the **center** of the quilt to maintain the zigzag look (see the purple circles), and the corner units with the **black Triangle Top** go around the **outside** of the design (see the red circles).

8. Referring to the Color Connector Square diagram below—and following the flow of the colors—add a 2½" (6.35cm) color connector square to one corner of the solid gray square of the adjoining block. If you add this connector before you lay out the blocks, you are then committed to the new color flow. Adding the connector AFTER you lay out (and approve) the color flow gives you the opportunity to rearrange the colors in the event they do not flow as you originally thought.

Color Connector Square

Triangle Unit Placement Diagram

9. Before sewing the blocks into the quilt top, stand back or take a photograph of the quilt so that you can identify any interrupted color flow or, perhaps, a twisted piece. It's better to do this step NOW rather than notice something AFTER the top is stitched together.

10. Once you are satisfied with the color placement for the quilt, stitch the blocks together into rows and the rows into the top. The corner units with the **white Triangle Top** go through the **center** of the quilt to maintain the zigzag look (see the purple circles in the Triangle Unit Placement Diagram under step 7). The corner units with the **black Triangle Top** go around the **outside** of the design (see the red circles in the Triangle Unit Placement Diagram under step 7).

11. Once the blocks are stitched together into the quilt top, give it a good press. Layer, baste, and quilt as desired. Bind using 2½" (6.35cm) x WOF strips of black. Add a hanging sleeve if desired. Don't forget to add the label.

Quilt Top

Quilt Top Assembly

About the Authors

THE AUTHORS

Linda J. Hahn is a multiple award-winning author, Janome Artisan Ambassador, fabric designer, pattern designer, long arm quilter, and sought-after speaker. Her books *New York Beauty Simplified* (AQS 2011) and *New York Beauty Diversified* (AQS 2013) won Bronze and Gold medals respectively in the Independent Publishers Living Now Book Awards. She has three other books, two of which have also won awards. Linda's first fabric collection, called Island Vibes by Banyan Batiks, was released in 2019. Her next collection, Carnivale, is scheduled for a 2020 release. Her work has been featured in many of your favorite quilting magazines. She was named the 2009 National Quilting Association Certified Teacher of the Year.

Linda recently moved to Palm Bay, Florida, where she lives with her husband, Allan. When not quilting, she can be found reading CIA/Black Ops novels while floating in her pool. She is a licensed Zumba instructor and also holds many specialty Zumba licenses.

Linda is available to visit with your guild, group, or retreat. Visit her website at *www.FrogHollow Designs.com* for more information.

Deborah G. Stanley is an independent designer, whose work has been published in many magazines, including *Quilt* magazine, *Love of Quilting*, *Modern Patchwork*, *American Quilter*, and *Quilter's World*. She has designed consumer projects for several fabric companies, including Banyan Batiks, Northcott, RJR, and Elizabeth's Studio. Her specialty is simple, easy-to-complete sewing and quilting projects, especially lap quilts and handbags. Using embellishments to "kick up" quilts is her favorite way to add personality. Her work has appeared in several of Linda Hahn's books, and her quilt "Five O'Clock Somewhere" was the cover quilt for Linda's book *Rock That Quilt Block: Hourglass* (AQS 2016).

Deb lives in New Jersey with her husband, Steve. When not quilting, she enjoys reading and crafts of all kinds, as well as practicing her newly acquired longarm skills.

THE COLLABORATION

Linda and Deborah have been "besties" for over 20 years. You may have seen them walking around the quilt show floor together. They enjoy traveling to different quilt show venues and taking classes together, although at times there have been some disagreements over whether the temperature in the room should be set at "chilly" or "arctic." They have collaborated on many of the magazine and fabric company designs, as well as on their own patterns. They are very successful at bouncing ideas and opinions off each other.

Their first book together was *New York Beauty Quilts Electrified* (Landauer Publishing, 2019).

Despite now being separated by miles, they speak to each other on the phone daily and arrange to meet for play or work dates.

Acknowledgments

We'd like to thank our piecing team—Sharon Dow, Nancy Rock, Janet Byard, and Allan Hahn—for their help in stitching the quilts in this book.

We'd also like to thank the following companies who provided us with our fabrics, threads and batting for these quilts: Banyan Batiks, Northcott, Hoffman California, Timeless Treasures, Elizabeth's Studio, Aurifil, and Mountain Mist.

We certainly can't forget to thank the team at Fox Chapel Publishing, including Tiffany Hill (acquisition editor), Katie Ocasio (editor), Wendy Reynolds (designer), and Mike Mihalo (photographer), for their support and for creating another beautiful book for us!

Resources

TOOLS AND MATERIALS

Rock That Quilt Block Kit
www.FrogHollowDesigns.com

Frog Hollow Designs
Foundation Paper
www.FrogHollowDesigns.com

Triangles on a Roll
www.FrogHollowDesigns.com

What's My Angle Tool
www.FrogHollowDesigns.com

Clover Chaco Liner
www.Clover-USA.com

THREAD

Aurifil
www.Aurifil.com

FABRICS

Northcott Silk
www.Northcott.com

Elizabeth's Studio
www.ElizabethsStudio.com

Banyan Batiks
www.Northcott.com

Hoffman California
*www.HoffmanCalifornia
Fabrics.net*

Timeless Treasures
www.TTFabrics.com

BATTING

Mountain Mist
www.MountainMistCrafts.com

To schedule a visit with Linda for your guild, group, or retreat, please contact:
Linda J. Hahn
lawnquilt@aol.com
321-586-4005
www.FrogHollowDesigns.com

PHOTO CREDITS

Photos of Linda Hahn's Carnivale fabric collection on pages 4–5, 8–9, 12 (bottom), and 13 (top) were photographed by Amber Petty for Banyan Batiks.
Clover Chaco Liner Pen Style image on page 10 provided by Clover Needlecraft, Inc.
Images from *www.Shutterstock.com*: Louella938 (rotary cutter 6); Katja El Sol Cemazar (bottom 11).

Index

Note: Page numbers in *italics* indicate projects.